Simply Delicious Cupcakes

By Carol Kicinski
Edited by Malory Speir

Copyright © 2007 – 2017 Simply Gluten Free, Inc. ALL RIGHTS RESERVED. Printed in the USA.

Simply Gluten Free is a registered trademark owned by Carol Kicinski. Any unauthorized copying, translation, duplication, importation or distribution, in whole or in part, by any means, including digital and electronic copying, storage or transmission, is a violation of applicable laws.

This book is organized into a convenient resource that contains new and existing recipes from Carol Kicinski's books and websites.

www.SimplyGluten-Free.com

ISBN: 978-0-9896612-3-2

About the Author

Carol Kicinski started her career in recipe development more than 20 years ago. Involving herself in the allergen-free arena, she founded Simply Gluten Free in 2007 as a gluten-free recipe and lifestyle blog. Her readers quickly made it one of the top gluten-free websites. Its purpose is to educate, assist and inspire those with celiac disease or sensitivity to gluten, dairy, nuts, grain or other allergenic elements. She even provides diet solutions for those with vegetarian, vegan, Paleo and raw preferences.

In June 2009, Carol became America's first gluten-free-only syndicated TV chef with a monthly segment on *Daytime*, a nationally syndicated show on NBC's WFLA Tampa Bay. The show currently reaches more than 80 million TV households monthly in America.

She has published more than 850 recipes in newspapers and magazines and was a monthly recipe contributor to Martha Stewart's *Whole Living* from 2011 to 2013. As a best-selling author, she has published four print cookbooks, including *Simply…Gluten Free Desserts*, *Simply…Gluten Free Quick Meals*, and *Simply Gluten Free 5 Ingredient Cookbook*.

In August 2012, Carol launched *Simply Gluten Free Magazine*, a print lifestyle magazine with a full digital version. It enjoys robust sales in thousands of supermarkets, health food stores and bookstores across America.

As a humanitarian and adventurer, Carol has assisted the National Red Cross around the world and was one of the first responders at Katrina's Central Command in New Orleans, Louisiana, assisting the troops. She's lived to tell about being charged by elephants and rhinos and has dived with Great White sharks in South Africa. Fun, interesting, accomplished, and adventurous, Carol's simplest passion is making "that great recipe" and then having someone else make it and love it!

This book is dedicated to cupcake lovers everywhere.
May each cupcake be a celebration you hold in your hand.

Table of Contents

05 Chocoholic's Collection

- 07 Carol's Black Forest Cupcakes
- 08 German Chocolate Cupcakes
- 10 Chocolate Cherry Flourless Mini Cupcakes
- 11 Mexican Chocolate Cupcakes
- 13 Chocolate Raspberry Cupcakes
- 14 Chocolate Ginger Bites
- 17 Mint Chocolate Chip Cupcakes
- 18 Peanut Butter-Filled Chocolate Cupcakes
- 20 Mini Cherry Brownie Cupcakes
- 21 Flourless Peanut Butter Chocolate Cupcakes

22 Classic Flavors

- 23 Very Vanilla Cupcakes
- 25 Jumbo Coconut Cupcakes
- 26 Famous Red Velvet Cupcakes
- 29 Strawberry Cupcakes
- 30 Strawberry Shortcake Cupcakes

32 Reinvented Recipes

- 33 Peanut Butter & Jelly Cupcakes
- 35 Salted Caramel Cupcakes
- 37 Cinnamon Apple Cupcakes
- 38 Cookies & Cream No-Bake Cupcakes

39 Scrumptious Seasons

- 40 Chocolate Almond Christmas Cupcakes
- 41 Bloody Surprise Cupcakes
- 42 Halloween Pumpkin Cupcakes
- 45 Fourth of July Blueberry Cupcakes
- 47 St. Paddy's Pistachio Cupcakes in a Jar
- 48 Easter Jelly Bean Cupcakes

49 Baked Beverages

- 50 Shirley Temple Cupcakes
- 53 Irish Coffee Cupcakes
- 54 Old Fashioned Cupcakes
- 57 Manhattan Cupcakes
- 58 Roy Rogers Cupcakes
- 61 Margarita Cupcakes

62 Dreamy Delights

- 63 Banana Cupcakes with Brown Sugar Frosting
- 64 Honey Orange Cupcakes
- 65 Italian Cream Cupcakes
- 67 Lemon-Lime Cupcakes
- 68 Julian's Carrot Cupcakes with Cream Cheese Frosting

70 Homemade from a Box

- 71 Snickerdoodle Cupcakes
- 72 Chocolate Coconut Pecan Cupcakes
- 73 Chocolate Strawberry Cupcakes
- 74 Flower Cupcakes
- 75 Graveyard Cupcakes
- 76 Cherry Heart Cupcakes

Introduction

I believe we all deserve treats in life.

When it comes to food, the most important thing is for it to taste great, and allergen-free food should be no exception. After decades of cooking gluten-free food for myself and non-gluten-free food for my husband and two sons, I can honestly say that regardless of whether or not something is "regular" or allergen-free, it *can* and *should* taste exactly the same. This is why my gluten-free recipes are not just "good for gluten-free," but are just plain good! Not just that, but even the recipes I make that are nut-free, egg-free, dairy-free, refined sugar-free, or vegan are all equal to their traditional counterparts.

This book is dedicated to one of my favorite treats: cupcakes! It includes recipes for some unique flavors as well as some classics and even holiday varieties. The cupcake recipes in this book work perfectly with traditional wheat flour or gluten-free flour, plus they are easily adaptable for other allergen-free diets.

In my opinion, cupcakes are the ultimate sharing food – you take them to parties and each one is a mini celebration. So, regardless of allergens or food preferences, why not share the celebration with everyone? With this book, you can. There is truly a cupcake for everyone! Enjoy!

xo,
Carol

If you are gluten-free or are making a recipe for someone who is, Carol's Gluten Free® All-Purpose Flour (on Amazon and simplygluten-free.com) is the recommended, but not required, gluten-free flour for all recipes. It is a pastry-quality flour that works cup-for-cup like regular flour.

Ingredient Key

Look for these symbols to see which recipes can easily be made to fit your dietary needs.*

 Dairy-Free

 Egg-Free

 Gluten-Free

 Nut-Free

 Refined Sugar-Free

 Vegan

*While Carol Kicinski may present many health ideas, concepts and recipes, none is meant to prescribe and all readers are directed to seek only professional doctor guidance for their health diagnosis, care, and instructions. It is specifically the readers' responsibility to confirm any recipe's suitability for their own healthful use.

Chocoholic's Collection

Chocolate. That one simple word can put a smile on your face and make an ordinary day extraordinary. These recipes are deeply rich, divinely decadent, and absolutely amazing.

This cupcake is based on Black Forest Cake. It is a lovely combination of chocolate, cherries and cream.

Carol's Black Forest Cupcakes

Makes 24 cupcakes

Ingredients:

For the Cupcakes:
½ cup unsalted butter, room temperature
1½ cups granulated sugar
2 large eggs, room temperature
1 teaspoon pure vanilla extract
1⅔ cups all-purpose flour (regular or gluten-free)
⅔ cup unsweetened cocoa powder
2 teaspoons baking powder
1 teaspoon kosher or fine sea salt
1½ cups milk
1 (14.5-ounce) can tart cherries, drained
1 (10-ounce) jar all-natural maraschino cherries, drained and liquid reserved, divided

For the Frosting:
1 cup heavy whipping cream
1 cup powdered sugar
½ teaspoon pure vanilla extract
Grated dark chocolate, for garnish

Directions:

Preheat the oven to 350°F. Line two standard muffin pans with paper liners.

Using an electric mixer, fitted with a paddle attachment, cream the butter and sugar on medium speed for about 5 minutes or until light and fluffy. Turn the mixer to low and add eggs, one at a time, until each egg is fully mixed in. Be sure to scrape down the sides of the bowl with each addition. Add vanilla extract and mix well.

Add flour, cocoa powder, baking powder, and salt in a separate large mixing bowl. Whisk to combine.

Turn the mixer on low and add the flour mixture and milk to the creamed butter, starting with one-third of the flour mixture, then half the milk, half the remaining flour mixture, the rest of the milk, and the rest of the flour. Mix until just combined. Remove the bowl from the mixer and scrape the sides and bottom of the bowl well with a spatula.

Put 2 tablespoons of batter into each muffin cup, add 3 tart cherries to each cup, and top with 2 more tablespoons of batter. Bake 20 to 25 minutes or until springy on the top. Let cool in the pan for 5 minutes.

Poke 8 holes in each cupcake, using a toothpick. Spoon about 1 teaspoon of reserved all-natural maraschino cherry liquid onto each cupcake and let it soak in. Transfer cupcakes to a wire rack to cool completely.

To make the frosting, whip the cream in a large bowl until soft peaks form. Add powdered sugar, vanilla, and 1 tablespoon of reserved maraschino cherry juice. Beat until stiff.

Frost cupcakes and garnish with an all-natural maraschino cherry and some grated chocolate.

German Chocolate Cupcakes

Makes 12 cupcakes

Ingredients:

For the Cupcakes:
- 1½ cups all-purpose flour (regular or gluten-free)
- ⅓ cup unsweetened cocoa powder
- 1 teaspoon baking soda
- ½ teaspoon kosher or fine sea salt
- 1 teaspoon instant espresso powder
- 1 cup granulated sugar
- 1 cup coconut milk (shake, then measure)
- ½ cup mayonnaise or vegan mayonnaise, such as Vegenaise™
- 2 teaspoons pure vanilla extract
- ½ teaspoon pure almond extract

For the Frosting:
- 1½ cups coconut flakes
- 1 cup pecans, chopped
- 4 cups powdered sugar, measured then sifted
- ¼ teaspoon kosher or fine sea salt
- ½ cup refined coconut oil, room temperature
- 2 teaspoons pure vanilla extract
- ½ teaspoon pure almond extract
- 4 to 6 tablespoons coconut milk

Directions:

Preheat the oven to 350°F. Line a 12-cup standard muffin pan with paper liners.

In a large mixing bowl, whisk together flour, cocoa powder, baking soda, salt, and espresso powder.

In a separate mixing bowl, whisk together sugar, coconut milk, mayo, and extracts. Add coconut milk mixture to dry ingredients and stir to combine. Divide batter evenly among prepared muffin cups, filling each cup about three-quarters full.

Bake 20 to 25 minutes or until the tops are slightly springy and a toothpick inserted in the center comes out clean. Leave the oven on. Let cool in the pan for 5 minutes, then transfer to a wire rack to finish cooling.

Prepare the frosting while the cupcakes cool. Place the coconut flakes and pecans on separate baking sheets. Toast in the oven until fragrant and lightly browned, about 5 minutes for coconut and about 10 minutes for pecans. Watch closely so they don't burn. Let cool while mixing the rest of the frosting.

In the bowl of an electric mixer, preferably fitted with a paddle attachment, combine powdered sugar, salt, coconut oil, and extracts. Starting with the mixer on low speed, blend until combined. Gradually increase speed to medium and add coconut milk, 1 tablespoon at a time, until it reaches the consistency of butter cream frosting. Turn the mixer to medium-high speed and continue to mix for 3 minutes.

Take a handful of toasted coconut flakes to use as garnish and set aside. Add the pecans and the rest of the coconut to the frosting and mix well with a spatula. You may need to add a bit more coconut milk to keep the frosting at a spreadable consistency. Frost cooled cupcakes, sprinkle with toasted coconut, and serve.

Coconut frosting.
Moist chocolate cake.
What more could you ask for?

Chocolate Cherry Flourless Mini Cupcakes

Makes 24 mini cupcakes

Ingredients:

24 all-natural maraschino cherries
6 ounces semisweet chocolate chips (1 cup)
½ cup unsalted butter
3 large eggs
¼ cup granulated sugar
1 tablespoon unsweetened cocoa powder, plus more for garnish
1½ tablespoons all-natural maraschino cherry liquid
⅛ teaspoon kosher or fine sea salt
½ cup heavy whipping cream
1 teaspoon pure vanilla extract
¼ cup powdered sugar

Directions:

Preheat the oven to 375°F. Line a 24-cup mini muffin pan with paper liners. Remove cherry stems, cut the cherries in half, and dry with paper towels.

Combine chocolate chips and butter in a large microwave-safe mixing bowl. Cook on high power until the butter is melted and the chocolate chips are very soft, about 2 minutes. Stir until smooth and glossy. Let cool slightly. Whisk in eggs, sugar, cocoa powder, cherry liquid, and salt. Ladle half the batter into the cups, place a cherry half in each cup, and fill with remaining batter, filling the cups almost full. Bake for 20 minutes, or until risen and the tops look dry. Let cupcakes cool in the pan.

Whip the cream with vanilla and powdered sugar. Top the cooled cupcakes with whipped cream, dust with a little cocoa powder, and top with the remaining all-natural maraschino cherry halves.

Mexican Chocolate Cupcakes

Makes 12 cupcakes

Ingredients:

For the Cupcakes:
- 1½ cups all-purpose flour (regular or gluten-free)
- ⅓ cup unsweetened cocoa powder
- 1 teaspoon baking soda
- ½ teaspoon kosher or fine sea salt
- 1 teaspoon ground cinnamon
- 1 cup granulated sugar
- 1 cup unflavored rice milk
- ½ cup chipotle mayonnaise or Chipotle Vegenaise™ (for less spicy, use half plus regular mayo)
- 2 teaspoons pure vanilla extract

For the Frosting:
- 1 cup vegetable shortening
- 2 teaspoons pure vanilla extract
- 2 teaspoons ground cinnamon
- ⅛ teaspoon kosher or fine sea salt
- 3 cups powdered sugar
- 2 to 4 tablespoons rice milk

Vegan mayo is my secret to moist, egg-free cupcakes. If you can't find Chipotle Vegenaise, mix chipotle chili powder into regular vegan mayo, to taste. If you aren't egg-free, you can use regular instead of vegan.

Directions:

Preheat the oven to 350°F. Line a standard muffin tin with paper cupcake liners. In a large bowl, whisk the flour, cocoa powder, baking soda, salt, and cinnamon.

In a separate mixing bowl, whisk together sugar, milk, mayo, and vanilla. Add wet ingredients to dry ingredients and stir or whisk to combine. Divide batter evenly among prepared muffin cups, filling each cup about three-quarters full. Bake 20 to 25 minutes or until tops are slightly springy and a toothpick inserted in the center comes out clean. Let cool in the pan for 5 minutes, then transfer to a wire rack to finish cooling.

Make frosting while cupcakes cool. Combine shortening, vanilla, cinnamon, salt, and powdered sugar in the bowl of a mixer. Start on low and gradually increase speed to medium. Beat until fluffy. Add milk, 1 tablespoon at a time, beating after each addition. Add just enough to make the frosting creamy and spreadable. Frost the cooled cupcakes and serve.

I created this recipe for my friend's baby shower. She was having a boy, so I chose flavors that represent boys.

Little boys don't tend to stay pristine for very long; they get scuffed and dirty and even muddy at times. They can also melt your heart in a nanosecond. So, of course these cupcakes had to feature chocolate.

I like to mix fruit with chocolate wherever I can but boys are not pure sweet, like a strawberry – they can have a little tart thrown in with the sweet, so raspberries instantly came to mind.

Unfortunately, a trip to the grocery store yielded only flavorless, un-ripe raspberries. Undeterred, I used no sugar added, freeze-dried raspberries instead.

Chocolate Raspberry Cupcakes

Makes 12 cupcakes

Ingredients:

For the Cupcakes:
1⅓ cups freeze-dried raspberries
¾ cup brown rice flour (preferably superfine)
¼ cup coconut flour
½ cup tapioca starch
½ cup unsweetened cocoa powder
1½ teaspoons baking powder
½ teaspoon baking soda
½ teaspoon kosher or fine sea salt
½ cup fat-free Greek yogurt
½ cup unsweetened apple sauce
½ cup low-fat 2% milk
3 large eggs
1 teaspoon pure vanilla extract
2 tablespoons grape seed or other neutral-tasting oil
1 cup coconut sugar

For the Frosting:
¾ cup dark agave nectar
3 large egg whites
⅛ teaspoon kosher or fine sea salt
2 teaspoons pure vanilla extract
6 tablespoons unsweetened cocoa powder

Directions:

Preheat the oven to 350°F. Line 12 standard muffin tins with paper liners.

Pick out 12 raspberries and set aside to garnish the cupcakes; keep them sealed in a plastic bag until ready to use. Place the rest in a plastic bag and roll with a rolling pin into crumbs.

In a large mixing bowl, whisk together the brown rice flour, coconut flour, tapioca starch, cocoa powder, baking powder, baking soda, salt, and crushed raspberries.

In another mixing bowl, whisk together the yogurt, apple sauce, milk, eggs, 1 teaspoon vanilla, oil, and coconut sugar. Add the wet ingredients to the dry ingredients and combine well. Divide the batter evenly among the muffin tins. Bake 25 minutes or until they feel firm to the touch and a toothpick inserted in the center comes out mostly clean. Let cool in the pan for 5 minutes, then transfer to a wire rack to finish cooling.

Meanwhile, make the frosting. Bring the agave to a boil in a heavy saucepan and continue to boil for 3 or 4 minutes, or until big bubbles form (225°F on a candy thermometer).

While the agave is cooking, beat the eggs whites with ⅛ teaspoon of salt until stiff peaks form. Carefully pour the agave into the egg whites with the mixer on low speed. After all the agave has been added, increase the speed to medium-high and continue beating until the frosting is completely cool, about 7 minutes. The frosting should be thick, glossy, and smooth. Sift the cocoa powder into the frosting and beat on medium-high just until the cocoa has been incorporated. Use a spatula to thoroughly combine.

To assemble, frost the cooled cupcakes and garnish with the reserved raspberries.

Chocolate Ginger Bites

Makes 36 mini cupcakes

Ingredients:

For the Cupcakes:
6 tablespoons unsalted butter, room temperature
⅔ cup granulated sugar
1 large egg, room temperature
½ teaspoon pure vanilla extract
1 (1-inch) cube fresh ginger, peeled and finely grated
1¼ cups all-purpose flour (regular or gluten-free)
1 teaspoon ground ginger
¼ teaspoon baking powder
¼ teaspoon baking soda
½ teaspoon kosher or fine sea salt
½ cup sour cream, room temperature
¼ cup crystallized ginger, finely chopped

For the Topping:
8 ounces semisweet or bittersweet chocolate chips
1 cup heavy whipping cream
Crystallized ginger, for garnish

Directions:

Preheat the oven to 350°F. Line 36 mini muffin cups with paper liners.

In the bowl of an electric mixer, fitted with a paddle attachment, cream the butter and sugar on medium speed until light and fluffy, about 3 minutes. Turn the speed to low, add the egg and mix well, scraping down the sides and bottom of the bowl with a spatula. Add the vanilla and grated fresh ginger and mix well.

In a separate large mixing bowl, whisk together the flour, ground ginger, baking powder, baking soda, and salt. With the mixer on low speed, add the flour mixture and sour cream to the creamed butter, starting with one-third of the flour mixture, then half the sour cream, half the remaining flour mixture, the rest of the sour cream, and the rest of the flour mixture. Mix until just combined. Remove the bowl from the mixer and scrape down the sides and bottom of the bowl well with a spatula. Fold in the chopped, crystallized ginger. Fill the prepared muffin cups about three-quarters full with batter.

Bake for 17 to 20 minutes, or until the tops are springy and a toothpick inserted in the center comes out clean. Let cool in the pans for 5 minutes, then transfer to a wire rack to cool completely.

Meanwhile, prepare the ganache. Place chocolate chips in a small bowl. In a small saucepan, heat the cream over medium heat until it just comes to a boil. Pour the cream over the chocolate and let sit 5 minutes. Whisk together until shiny and smooth.

When the cupcakes are cool, dip the tops into the chocolate ganache and let the ganache cool. Garnish the cupcakes with thin strips of crystallized ginger.

Mint Chocolate Chip Cupcakes

Makes 36 mini cupcakes

Ingredients:

For the Cupcakes:
8 tablespoons unsalted butter, room temperature
1 cup granulated sugar
2 large eggs, room temperature
1 teaspoon pure vanilla extract
1 to 2 teaspoons pure mint extract
3 cups all-purpose flour (regular or gluten-free)
1 tablespoon baking powder
¼ teaspoon baking soda
½ teaspoon kosher or fine sea salt
1½ cups buttermilk, room temperature
5 or 6 drops of green food coloring
4 ounces dark chocolate, chopped

For the Frosting:
2 large egg whites
½ cup granulated sugar
Pinch of kosher or fine sea salt
1 cup unsalted butter, room temperature, cut into tablespoon-sized pieces
1 teaspoon pure vanilla extract
3 ounces dark chocolate, melted and cooled

Directions:

Preheat the oven to 325°F. Insert paper liners into 36 mini muffin cups.

Add butter and sugar in the bowl of an electric mixer fitted with a paddle attachment. Combine on medium speed for about 3 minutes or until light and fluffy. Turn mixer to low and add eggs, one at a time, mixing until each egg is fully combined. Scrape down the sides of the bowl with each addition. Add vanilla and mint extracts and mix well.

Add flour, baking powder, baking soda, and salt in a separate large mixing bowl. Whisk to combine. Turn the mixer on low and add flour mixture and buttermilk to the creamed butter, starting with one-third of the flour mixture, then half the buttermilk, half the remaining flour, the rest of the buttermilk mixture, and the rest of the flour mixture. Mix until just combined. Remove the bowl from the mixer and scrape the sides and bottom of the bowl well with a large spatula. To get the mixture to a light green shade, add a couple drops of food coloring at a time until it looks like mint chip ice cream. Fold in the chopped chocolate.

Pour the batter into muffin cups, about two-thirds full. Bake 12 to 17 minutes or until the tops are springy and a toothpick inserted in the center comes out clean. Let cool in pan 5 minutes, then transfer to a wire rack to cool completely.

For the frosting, combine egg, sugar, and salt in a heatproof bowl of a stand mixer. Place over a pan containing 1 to 2 inches of simmering water. (The bottom of the mixing bowl should not touch the hot water.) Whisk constantly, either by hand or with a handheld mixer, until the mixture feels warm to the touch and the sugar is melted, about 2 minutes. Rub a bit between your forefinger and thumb to feel if it is smooth.

Attach the bowl to the mixer, fitted with a whisk attachment, and beat until the mixture is glossy, fluffy, and completely cool, about 10 minutes. With the mixer on medium-low speed, add the butter, a few tablespoons at a time, mixing well after each addition. Once the butter has been fully incorporated, add the vanilla and mix well. Add the cooled melted chocolate and mix well. With a spatula, scrape the sides and bottom of the bowl and stir for 1 to 2 minutes to remove any air bubbles. The frosting should be completely smooth. If the frosting starts to curdle or separate after adding the butter, just keep beating it until it is smooth again. Frost the cooled cupcakes.

Peanut Butter-Filled Chocolate Cupcakes

Makes 24 cupcakes

Ingredients:

For the Cupcakes:
1¾ cup all-purpose flour (regular or gluten-free)
1½ teaspoons baking soda
½ teaspoon kosher or fine sea salt
¾ cup unsweetened cocoa powder
2 tablespoons instant espresso powder
½ cup boiling water
1 cup buttermilk
12 tablespoons unsalted butter, room temperature
1½ cups granulated sugar
3 large eggs, room temperature
1 teaspoon pure vanilla extract

For the Filling:
1 cup creamy peanut butter
4 tablespoons unsalted butter, room temperature
⅔ cup powdered sugar

For the Ganache:
8 ounces semisweet or bittersweet chocolate chips
1 cup heavy whipping cream

Directions:

For the Cupcakes: Preheat the oven to 350°F. Line 24 standard-size muffin cups with paper liners.

In a mixing bowl, whisk flour, baking soda, and salt, and set aside. In a separate bowl, combine cocoa powder and espresso powder and add boiling water. Whisk until a smooth paste forms. Add buttermilk and whisk until well combined.

In the bowl of an electric mixer, fitted with a paddle attachment, cream together butter and sugar on medium speed until light and fluffy, about 3 minutes. Turn speed to low and add eggs, one at a time, mixing well and scraping down the sides of the bowl after each addition. Add vanilla and mix well. Add one-third of the flour mixture, half the buttermilk mixture, half the remaining flour mixture, the rest of the buttermilk, and the rest of the flour mixture. Mix until just combined. With a spatula, scrape down the sides and bottom of the bowl, making sure the batter is well mixed. Divide batter into muffin cups, filling each about two-thirds full.

Bake for 20 to 25 minutes, or until the tops are springy and a toothpick inserted in the center comes out clean. Let cool in the pans for 10 minutes, then transfer to a wire rack to cool completely.

For the Filling: In the bowl of an electric mixer, fitted with the paddle attachment, beat the peanut butter with the butter on medium speed until creamy. Turn off the mixer and sift in the powdered sugar. Turn the mixer on again, starting on low speed, and slowly increasing to medium, and beat until fluffy, about 2 minutes. Reserve 3 tablespoons of the filling to top the cupcakes, and scoop the rest into a pastry bag fitted with a star tip or into a small plastic storage bag with ¼ inch cut off one corner.

When the cupcakes have cooled, take the end of a wooden spoon and gently press down in the center of each cupcake, wiggling the spoon back and forth to make a hole about 1 inch in diameter. Gently pipe the peanut butter filling into each cupcake. Scrape any filling off the top of the cupcakes so the tops are flat.

For the Ganache: Place chocolate chips in a small bowl. In a small saucepan, heat the cream over medium heat until it just comes to a boil. Pour the cream over the chocolate and let sit 5 minutes. Whisk together until shiny and smooth. Dip the top of each filled cupcake into the ganache, letting the excess drip back into the pan. Let sit 5 minutes, then dip again. Let sit another 10 minutes, until the ganache has firmed. Spoon the remaining 3 tablespoons of peanut butter filling into a pastry bag fitted with a star tip and pipe a little star garnish on top of each cupcake.

Mini Cherry Brownie Cupcakes

Makes 48 mini cupcakes

Ingredients:

For the Cupcakes:
1 (10-ounce) jar all-natural maraschino cherries, drained, reserving 5 tablespoons of syrup
8 ounces bittersweet chocolate chips
1 cup unsalted butter
1 teaspoon pure vanilla extract
¾ cup granulated sugar
3 large eggs, beaten
1½ cups ground almonds
¼ teaspoon kosher or fine sea salt
Ganache (recipe below) or 1 cup whipped cream
48 all-natural maraschino cherries, drained and patted dry, for garnish

For the Chocolate Ganache:
4 ounces semisweet chocolate chips
½ cup heavy whipping cream
3 tablespoons reserved cherry syrup

Directions:

Preheat the oven to 350°F. Insert paper liners in 48 mini muffin cups. Pat cherries dry and chop roughly. Set aside.

Melt chocolate chips and butter in a bowl in the microwave for 2½ to 3 minutes, until the butter is fully melted and the chips are almost melted. Stir until all the chocolate is melted and the mixture is smooth and glossy. Stir in the vanilla, sugar, and 2 tablespoons reserved cherry syrup. Let cool slightly.

Beat in the eggs, almonds, salt, and chopped cherries. Divide batter between the prepared muffin tins, filling the tins almost full. Bake 10 to 14 minutes or until the tops are set and slightly firm to the touch but the insides are still soft. Do not over-bake. Let cool in the pan for 5 minutes, then transfer to a wire rack to finish cooling.

For whipped cream, add 1 to 2 tablespoons reserved cherry syrup and mix well. Pipe or dollop it on just before serving and top with a cherry.

For chocolate ganache, pour chocolate chips into a small bowl. Heat the cream and cherry syrup in a small pan over medium-high heat until it just comes to a boil. Pour the hot cream mixture over the chocolate chips and let sit for 5 minutes. Stir until smooth and glossy. Let sit 10 to 15 minutes, then spoon over the brownies. Top each with a cherry and refrigerate at least 30 minutes to firm.

Flourless Peanut Butter Chocolate Cupcakes

Makes 12 cupcakes

Ingredients:

1¼ cups creamy peanut butter (or sunflower seed butter)
1 cup brown sugar, packed
½ cup milk or dairy-free milk of choice
4 large eggs, separated
1 tablespoon pure vanilla extract
1 teaspoon baking soda
½ teaspoon kosher or fine sea salt
1 teaspoon fresh lemon juice
2 cups semisweet or dairy-free mini chocolate chips, divided
¾ cup heavy cream or full-fat canned coconut milk

Directions:

Preheat the oven to 350°F. Place paper cupcake liners in a 12-cup standard muffin tin.

In a mixer, beat peanut butter, sugar, milk, egg yolks, vanilla, baking soda, salt, and lemon juice.

With clean beaters, whip the egg whites until stiff peaks form. Stir a large spoonful of egg whites into the batter. Gently fold in the rest of the egg whites until the mixture is no longer streaky. Fold in 1 cup of chocolate chips. Divide the batter evenly among the prepared muffin tins. Bake for 15 to 20 minutes or until a toothpick inserted into the center comes out clean. Let cool in the pan for 5 minutes, then transfer to a wire rack to finish cooling.

Place the remaining 1 cup of chocolate chips in a heat-proof bowl. Bring the cream to almost a boil in a small saucepan. Pour the hot cream over the chocolate chips and let sit for 5 minutes. Stir until the mixture is smooth and glossy. Drizzle the chocolate mixture over the cooled cupcakes and serve.

Classic Flavors

Although these recipes are original, their flavors are classics. From vanilla to strawberry to red velvet, these flavors are traditional, yet sensational!

Very Vanilla Cupcakes

Makes 18 cupcakes

Ingredients:

8 tablespoons unsalted butter, room temperature
1 cup granulated sugar
2 large eggs, room temperature
1 tablespoon pure vanilla bean paste or pure vanilla extract
3 cups all-purpose flour (regular or gluten-free)
1 tablespoon baking powder
¼ teaspoon baking soda
½ teaspoon kosher or fine sea salt
1½ cups buttermilk
Frosting and decorations of choice

Directions:

Preheat the oven to 325°F. Insert paper liners into 18 standard muffin cups.

In the bowl of an electric mixer, fitted with a paddle attachment, cream the butter and sugar on medium speed until light and fluffy, about 3 minutes. Turn speed to low and add eggs, one at a time, mixing well until each egg is fully incorporated. Scrape down the sides of the bowl after each addition. Add vanilla and mix well.

In a separate bowl, whisk to combine flour, baking powder, baking soda, and salt. Turn mixer on low and add the flour mixture and buttermilk to the creamed butter, starting with one-third of the flour mixture, half the buttermilk, half the remaining flour mixture, the rest of the buttermilk, and the rest of the flour mixture. Mix until just combined. Scrape down the sides and bottom of the bowl. Pour into muffin cups, about two-thirds full.

Bake 20 to 25 minutes, or until the tops are springy to the touch and a toothpick inserted in the center comes out clean. Let cool in the pans for 5 minutes, then transfer to a wire rack to cool completely.

  When the cupcakes are completely cool, frost and decorate as desired.

I make these as big, oversized cupcakes because I think it adds to their charm. But if you prefer to make yours smaller, just fill the baking liners only two-thirds full. This will give you about 36 cupcakes.

Jumbo Coconut Cupcakes

Makes 24 large cupcakes

Ingredients:

For the Cupcakes:
1 tablespoon fresh lemon juice
1 cup coconut milk (shake can before measuring)
¾ pound unsalted butter, room temperature
2 cups granulated sugar
6 large eggs, room temperature
1½ teaspoons pure vanilla extract
1½ teaspoons pure almond extract
3 cups all-purpose flour (regular or gluten-free)
1 teaspoon baking powder
½ teaspoon baking soda
½ teaspoon kosher or fine sea salt
14 ounces sweetened shredded coconut

For the Frosting:
1 pound cream cheese, room temperature
¾ pound unsalted butter, room temperature
Pinch of kosher or fine sea salt
1 teaspoon pure vanilla extract
½ teaspoon pure almond extract
1½ pounds powdered sugar

Directions:

Preheat the oven to 325°F. Spray 24 large-size muffin cups lightly with nonstick cooking spray (regular or gluten-free) and insert cupcake liners in each cup.

In a small mixing bowl, stir the lemon juice into the coconut milk and let sit for 5 minutes. Don't worry if it starts to look curdled, this is normal.

Combine butter and sugar in the bowl of an electric mixer, fitted with a paddle attachment. Blend on medium speed for about 5 minutes or until very light and fluffy. Turn the speed to low and add the eggs, one at a time, mixing well until each egg is fully incorporated. Be sure to scrape down the sides of the bowl with a spatula after each addition. Add the vanilla and almond extracts and mix well.

Add the flour, baking powder, baking soda, and salt in a separate large mixing bowl. Whisk to combine. Turn the mixer on low speed and add the flour mixture and coconut milk mixture to the creamed butter, starting with one-third of the flour mixture, then half the coconut milk mixture, half the remaining flour mixture, the rest of the coconut milk mixture, and the rest of the flour mixture. Mix until just combined. Remove the bowl from the mixer and scrape the sides and bottom of the bowl with a large spatula. Fold in half of the shredded coconut. Pour batter to the top of each prepared muffin cup. Tap the pans on the counter three times to settle the batter.

Bake 25 to 30 minutes, rotating the pans halfway through the baking time, until springy on the top and a toothpick inserted in the center comes out clean. Let cupcakes cool in the pan for 10 minutes, then transfer to a wire rack to cool completely. If the cupcakes seem difficult to remove, you may have to run a small offset spatula gently around the edges to get the cupcakes out of the pan without breaking the tops.

Make the frosting while the cupcakes are baking and cooling. Combine cream cheese, butter, salt, and vanilla and almond extracts in the bowl of an electric mixer, fitted with a paddle attachment. Blend on medium speed. Turn off the mixer, sift in the powdered sugar, turn the mixer back on, and mix on low speed until smooth.

Put the frosting in the refrigerator to firm up while the cupcakes finish baking and cooling. Frost cupcakes when they have completely cooled.

Famous Red Velvet Cupcakes

Makes 24 cupcakes

Ingredients:

For the Cupcakes:
¾ pound unsalted butter, room temperature
2½ cups granulated sugar
3 large eggs, room temperature
1½ teaspoons pure vanilla extract
4 ounces red food coloring
3½ cups all-purpose flour (regular or gluten-free)
¼ cup unsweetened cocoa powder, plus more for dusting
1½ teaspoons kosher or fine sea salt
1½ cups buttermilk
1½ teaspoons apple cider vinegar
1½ teaspoons baking powder

For the Frosting:
12 ounces cream cheese, room temperature
16 tablespoons unsalted butter, room temperature
¼ teaspoon kosher or fine sea salt
1 teaspoon pure vanilla extract
1 pound powdered sugar

Directions:

Preheat the oven to 350°F. Line 24 standard muffin cups with paper liners.

Combine butter and sugar in the bowl of an electric mixer, fitted with a paddle attachment, and blend on medium speed until very light and fluffy, about 5 minutes. Turn the speed to low and add eggs, one at a time, mixing well until each egg is fully incorporated. Scrape down the sides of the bowl with a spatula after each addition. Add vanilla and red food coloring and mix well.

Add flour, cocoa powder, and salt in a separate mixing bowl and whisk to combine.

Turn the mixer on low and add the flour mixture and buttermilk to the creamed butter, starting with one-third of the flour mixture, then half the buttermilk, half the remaining flour mixture, the rest of the buttermilk, and the rest of the flour mixture. Mix until just combined. Remove bowl from mixer and scrape down the sides and bottom of the bowl well with a large spatula.

Mix apple cider vinegar and baking soda in a separate small bowl. Add to the batter and mix well. Divide batter among the cups and tap the pans on the counter a couple times to settle the batter.

Bake 20 to 25 minutes, turning the pans halfway through the baking time, until springy on top and a toothpick inserted in the center comes out clean. Let cool in the pans for 10 minutes, then transfer to a wire rack to cool completely.

Make the frosting while the cupcakes are baking and cooling. In the bowl of an electric mixer, fitted with a paddle attachment, blend together cream cheese, butter, salt, and vanilla extract on medium speed. Turn off the mixer and sift in the powdered sugar. Turn the mixer to low speed and mix until smooth. Frost the cooled cupcakes and dust with cocoa powder.

Who knows why someone decided to dump a bunch of red food coloring into cake batter, but I'm sure glad they did. I decided to honor this fabulously famous cake with a cupcake version!

This recipe is a double strawberry whammy – strawberries in the cupcakes and the frosting! Resist the temptation to overload the frosting with too many strawberries; they will exude liquid that will make the frosting difficult to work with.

Strawberry Cupcakes

Makes 12 cupcakes

Ingredients:

For the Cupcakes:
1½ cups all-purpose flour (regular or gluten-free)
1 teaspoon baking powder
½ teaspoon baking soda
½ teaspoon kosher or fine sea salt
1 tablespoon grape seed or other neutral-tasting oil
1 cup granulated sugar
1 cup milk, dairy-free milk, or water (I like to use half coconut milk and half water)
1 tablespoon fresh lemon juice
2 teaspoons pure vanilla extract
1 cup fresh strawberries, very finely chopped

For the Frosting:
¼ cup cream cheese (or dairy-free alternative)
¼ cup unsalted butter (or dairy-free alternative)
1 tablespoon coconut oil
¼ teaspoon kosher or fine sea salt
2 teaspoons pure vanilla extract
1 tablespoon fresh lemon juice
¼ cup finely chopped strawberries
4 to 5 cups (or more) powdered sugar*

*Depending on the type of powdered sugar you use and the humidity, the amount will vary.

Directions:

Preheat the oven to 350°F. Line 12 standard-sized muffin cups with paper liners.

Combine the flour, baking powder, baking soda, and salt in a mixing bowl and whisk to combine. In another mixing bowl, whisk together the oil, sugar, milk, lemon juice, and vanilla until smooth. Add the wet ingredients to the dry ingredients and stir to combine. Let sit 5 minutes to thicken. Stir in the strawberries and divide the batter among the prepared cups, filling each cup almost full. Bake 30 to 35 minutes or until golden brown, the cupcakes feel firm to the touch, and a toothpick inserted into the center comes out clean. The strawberries will make these cupcakes very moist. Let cool in the pan 5 minutes, then transfer to a wire rack to finish cooling.

While the cupcakes cool, make the frosting. Combine the cream cheese, butter, and coconut oil in a mixing bowl of an electric mixer, preferably fitted with a paddle attachment, and beat at medium-high speed until smooth. You may have to scrape down the sides of the bowl a couple times to ensure the mixture is completely smooth. Add salt, vanilla, lemon juice, and strawberries and mix to combine. Sift in 4 cups of powdered sugar and mix, starting on low speed, to combine. You may need to add more sugar because you want the frosting to be the consistency of either stiffly whipped cream or butter cream frosting. Refrigerate the frosting for about 10 minutes before frosting the cupcakes.

Frost the cupcakes and refrigerate until serving time. If desired, garnish with strawberry slices and mint leaves.

Strawberry Shortcake Cupcakes

Makes 12 cupcakes

Ingredients:

1½ cups all-purpose flour (regular or gluten-free)
1 teaspoon baking powder
¼ teaspoon baking soda
½ teaspoon kosher or fine sea salt
½ cup unsalted butter, room temperature
1⅓ cups granulated sugar, divided
3 large eggs

2 teaspoons plus 1 tablespoon pure vanilla extract, divided
½ cup sour cream, room temperature
2 pints fresh strawberries
1 tablespoon fresh lemon juice
2 cups cold heavy cream
3 tablespoons powdered sugar

Directions:

Preheat oven to 350°F. Line a standard muffin tin with paper cupcake liners.

Combine the flour, baking powder, baking soda, and salt in a mixing bowl and whisk.

In the bowl of an electric mixer, preferably fitted with a paddle attachment, beat the butter and 1 cup sugar on high speed for 5 minutes. Beat in the eggs, one at a time, scraping down the sides of the bowl after each addition. Beat in 2 teaspoons vanilla extract.

Turn the mixer to low, add half the flour mixture, then the sour cream, and finally the remaining flour. Mix until combined. With a spatula, scrape the sides and bottom of the mixing bowl to ensure all ingredients are well combined. Divide the batter evenly into the prepared muffin tins. Bake for 18 to 20 minutes or until a toothpick inserted into the center comes out clean. Let cool in the pan for 5 minutes, then transfer to a wire rack to finish cooling.

While the cupcakes are baking and cooling, reserve a few strawberries for garnish, slice the rest, and mix with ⅓ cup sugar and the lemon juice. Let sit for 15 to 20 minutes, tossing occasionally. Lightly mash the strawberries with a fork.

Cut a hole about as wide as a quarter and about ½ inch or so deep into the top of each cooled cupcake. Spoon the strawberry mixture into the holes. (You can reserve some of the strawberries and syrup to drizzle on top of the frosted cupcakes, if desired.)

Whip the cream with the remaining 1 tablespoon of vanilla and the powdered sugar until it forms peaks. Frost each cupcake with the whipped cream. Slice the reserved strawberries and garnish.

Reinvented Recipes

These cupcakes are reminiscent of some very familiar flavors. From childhood staples like PB&J to more common ingredients like caramel, these recipes give old favorites a new form.

Peanut Butter & Jelly Cupcakes

Makes 12 cupcakes

Ingredients:

For the Cupcakes:
- 4 large eggs, separated
- ½ teaspoon cream of tartar
- Pinch of kosher or fine sea salt
- 3 tablespoons granulated sugar
- ¾ cup creamy peanut butter
- 3 tablespoons vegetable oil
- 1 teaspoon pure vanilla extract
- ½ cup ground almonds (meal)
- 1 teaspoon baking soda
- ¼ cup good-quality strawberry jam

For the Frosting:
- 8 ounces cream cheese, room temperature
- ¾ cup unsalted butter, room temperature
- 1 teaspoon pure vanilla extract
- 1½ cups powdered sugar, sifted
- 3 heaping tablespoons good-quality strawberry jam

Directions:

Preheat the oven to 350°F. Line 12 standard muffin cups with paper liners.

Using an electric mixer on high speed, whip egg whites, salt, and cream of tartar until soft peaks appear. Keep the mixer running and add sugar, 1 tablespoon at a time, until stiff peaks form.

Add egg yolks to peanut butter, oil, and vanilla in a separate bowl. Beat with a mixer until very smooth. Add almonds and baking soda. Mix well. Add egg whites and mix with a spatula until batter is no longer streaky.

Pour about 2 tablespoons of batter in the bottom of each muffin cup. Add 1 teaspoon of jam to each cup and top with remaining batter. Bake 20 to 25 minutes, until cupcakes have risen, are golden brown, and springy to the touch. Let cool completely on a wire rack before frosting.

For the frosting, blend cream cheese, butter, and vanilla in the bowl of an electric mixer. Turn mixer off and add powdered sugar. Turn mixer on low and blend, increasing speed until the mixture is very smooth. Add jam and mix until just combined. Frost the cooled cupcakes and serve.

I used to make caramel the traditional way, melting sugar until it became deep amber in color, being careful not to cause crystals, whisking in cream and butter and risking fourth degree burns.

But lately I have taken to making caramel by simply boiling agave with some cream for 5 minutes, whisking in the butter, and letting it cool.

And, using agave means these ooey-gooey cupcakes are refined-sugar free!

Salted Caramel Cupcakes

Makes 12 cupcakes

Ingredients:

For the Agave Caramel:
1 cup raw blue agave nectar
½ cup heavy cream
4 tablespoons cold unsalted butter
1 teaspoon kosher or fine sea salt

For the Caramel Frosting:
6 tablespoons coconut sugar
3 large eggs whites
1 cup unsalted butter, room temperature
1 teaspoon pure vanilla extract
5 tablespoons agave caramel

For the Cupcakes:
1½ cups all-purpose flour (regular or gluten-free)
1½ teaspoon baking powder
½ teaspoon kosher or fine sea salt
1 cup coconut sugar
1 large egg
¾ cup milk
1 tablespoon pure vanilla extract
½ cup grape seed or other neutral-tasting vegetable oil
16 to 18 teaspoons agave caramel

Directions:

To make the agave caramel, combine agave and cream in a large saucepan (use one bigger than you think you will need) and bring to a boil. Let boil for 5 minutes, stirring occasionally. Remove from heat and whisk in butter, 1 tablespoon at a time. Transfer to a bowl or jar and let cool completely. If it gets too thick to work with, heat it slightly.

To make the frosting, combine coconut sugar with egg whites in a heatproof bowl of a stand mixer and set over a pan of simmering water. Whisk by hand until the mixture is warm and the sugar has dissolved, 2 to 3 minutes.

Attach the mixing bowl to the stand mixer fitted with a whisk attachment. Beat, starting on low then increasing the speed to medium-high, until the mixture is thick, fluffy, glossy, and completely cool, about 6 minutes. Reduce speed to medium-low and add butter, 1 tablespoon at a time, beating well after each addition. Add vanilla and caramel and beat on medium-high until the caramel is fully incorporated. Remove the bowl from the mixer and stir the frosting vigorously with a spatula to knock out some of the air and make sure the caramel is fully mixed in. Let sit at room temperature.

To make the cupcakes, preheat the oven to 350°F. Line a standard muffin tin with paper liners.

Combine flour, baking powder, and salt in a mixing bowl and whisk. In another mixing bowl, whisk together coconut sugar with egg, milk, vanilla, and oil. Add flour mixture to the wet ingredients and whisk until smooth and it starts to thicken slightly. Divide batter among prepared muffin cups and bake 18 to 22 minutes or until they are golden brown and puffed, the tops spring back slightly, and a toothpick inserted into the center comes out clean. Let cool in the pan 5 minutes, then transfer to a wire rack to finish cooling.

Once the cupcakes are completely cool, cut a cone-shaped piece about 1 inch in diameter from the top of the cupcakes. Insert your finger into the holes and widen the bottom a bit. Spoon in about 1 teaspoon of the caramel, cut the tip off the cone, and place the top over the caramel. Spread or pipe the frosting on top and drizzle with a little bit of caramel. Cupcakes can be stored in the refrigerator but are best served at room temperature.

Cinnamon Apple Cupcakes

Makes 12 cupcakes

Ingredients:

For the Cupcakes:
1 large apple (I prefer Fuji), chopped
½ cup plus 2 tablespoons melted coconut oil*
½ cup coconut sugar
¼ cup plus 1 tablespoon agave nectar
½ cup coconut flour
½ teaspoon ground cinnamon
½ teaspoon kosher or fine sea salt
¼ teaspoon baking soda
6 large eggs
1 tablespoon pure vanilla extract

For the Frosting:
¾ cup agave nectar
1 teaspoon ground cinnamon
3 large egg whites
⅛ teaspoon kosher or fine sea salt
1 tablespoon pure vanilla extract

* Be sure to use refined coconut oil, unless you want a coconut flavor to your cupcakes.

Directions:

Preheat the oven to 350°F. Line a standard muffin tin with paper cupcake liners.

Combine chopped apple, 2 tablespoons melted coconut oil, coconut sugar, and 1 tablespoon agave in a medium saucepan and bring to a boil. Let simmer 8 to 10 minutes or until the apples are soft but still retain their shape. Let cool.

In a mixing bowl, whisk together coconut flour, cinnamon, salt, and baking soda. In a separate bowl, whisk together eggs, remaining ½ cup coconut oil, remaining ¼ cup cinnamon agave, and vanilla. Add coconut flour mixture to liquid ingredients and whisk well until smooth. Stir in the apple mixture. Divide batter among muffin cups, filling almost full. Bake 20 to 25 minutes or until cupcakes feel firm to the touch and a toothpick inserted into the center comes out clean. Let cool in the pan. While the cupcakes cool, prepare the frosting.

For the frosting, pour the agave and cinnamon into a high-sided pan. (Use a pan a lot larger than you think you will need, as the agave increases in size as it boils.) Bring to a boil. Continue to boil for 3 minutes. It should have large bubbles or reach 225°F on a candy thermometer.

Combine egg whites and salt and beat with a mixer on low until foamy, then increase the speed to high and beat until stiff peaks form. Turn the mixer to low, carefully pour in the agave, then turn the mixer back to high and beat until cool, about 7 minutes. Beat in the vanilla.

Generously frost the cooled cupcakes and top with apple slices for garnish, if desired.

Cookies & Cream No-Bake Cupcakes

Makes 12 cupcakes

Ingredients:

21 chocolate sandwich cream cookies (such as Oreos™ or gluten-free Kinnitoos™)
1 cup heavy cream
8 ounces cream cheese, softened
½ cup granulated sugar
1 teaspoon pure vanilla extract

Directions:

Line a standard 12-cup muffin pan with paper liners.

Take 3 of the cookies, cut them in quarters for garnish, and set aside. Place 12 cookies in a plastic freezer bag and pound them with a rolling pin until they turn into fine crumbs. Divide the crumbs among the muffin cups and press down firmly and evenly. Place the remaining cookies in the bag and break them up so that there are bigger pieces of cookie as well as some crumbs.

Whip the cream on high speed with a hand-held mixer until stiff peaks form. Place the cream cheese, sugar, and vanilla in a large mixing bowl and beat on high speed until smooth and well blended. Fold in the whipped cream and the crushed cookie pieces. Spoon the mixture into the muffin cups. Place one of the quartered cookies on top of each cheesecake. Refrigerate until serving, at least 5 minutes or up to a day ahead.

Scrumptious Seasons

Cupcakes are great any time of the year. And since there are endless ways to decorate a cupcake, they are the perfect treat to bake for the holidays.

Chocolate Almond Christmas Cupcakes

Makes 12 cupcakes

Ingredients:

- 1 cup canned coconut milk
- 2 tablespoons pure vanilla extract, divided
- 1¾ cups chocolate chips (regular or dairy-free), divided
- 2½ cups blanched almond flour
- 2 teaspoons baking powder
- ½ teaspoon kosher or fine sea salt
- 3 large eggs, separated
- ¼ cup grape seed or other neutral-tasting oil
- ¾ cup agave nectar
- ½ teaspoon pure almond extract
- ½ cup all-natural maraschino cherries, drained, dried and roughly chopped
- 12 all-natural maraschino cherries with stems, for garnish
- Slivered almonds, for garnish

Directions:

Preheat the oven to 325°F. Line a standard 12-cup muffin pan with paper liners.

Bring milk just to a boil in a saucepan. Turn off the heat and stir in 1 tablespoon vanilla and 1¼ cups chocolate chips. Let sit for 5 minutes. Stir until smooth and glossy. Pour into a bowl and refrigerate until cold, at least 30 minutes.

In a mixing bowl, whisk together almond flour, baking powder, and salt. Put egg yolks in one mixing bowl and egg whites in another. Beat egg whites on high speed until stiff peaks form. Add the remaining tablespoon of vanilla to the yolks along with oil, agave, and almond extract. Beat on high speed until it becomes thicker and lighter in color, about 2 minutes. Take a scoop of the beaten egg whites and stir into the yolk mixture. Fold the remaining whites into the yolks. Add the flour mixture and fold in until fully combined. Add remaining ½ cup chocolate chips and the chopped cherries and mix. Divide batter among muffin cups and bake for 30 minutes or until the cupcakes are browned, feel springy to the touch, and a toothpick inserted in the center comes out clean. Let cool in the pan for 15 minutes, then transfer to a wire rack to finish cooling.

When the frosting is cold, whip it on high speed with a hand-held mixer until fluffy. Frost the cooled cupcakes and garnish with a cherry and a couple almond slices.

Bloody Surprise Cupcakes

Makes 12 cupcakes

Ingredients:

For the Cupcakes:
- 1½ cups all-purpose flour (regular or gluten-free)
- ⅓ cup unsweetened cocoa powder
- 1 teaspoon baking soda
- ½ teaspoon kosher or fine sea salt
- 1 cup granulated sugar
- 1 cup milk or dairy-free milk
- ½ cup mayonnaise or vegan mayonnaise
- 2 teaspoons pure vanilla extract

For the Filling:
- 24 ounces frozen dark sweet cherries (do not thaw)
- ⅔ cup granulated sugar
- 2 tablespoons fresh lemon juice

For the Frosting:
- 1½ cups semisweet or dairy-free chocolate chips
- 1 cup vegetable shortening
- 3 cups powdered sugar
- 1 teaspoon pure vanilla extract
- 2-5 tablespoons milk or dairy-free milk
- Gummy worms (regular, gluten-free, and/or vegan)

Directions:

For the Cupcakes: Preheat the oven to 350°F. Line a standard 12-cup muffin pan with paper liners.

In a large mixing bowl, whisk flour, cocoa powder, baking soda, and salt. In a separate mixing bowl, whisk sugar, milk, mayonnaise, and vanilla. Add wet ingredients to the dry and stir to combine. Divide batter evenly among the prepared muffin cups. Bake 20 to 25 minutes or until the tops of the cupcakes spring back when lightly touched and a toothpick inserted in the center comes out clean. Let cool in the pan for 5 minutes, then transfer to a wire rack to finish cooling.

For the Filling: Chop the frozen cherries. Place in a small pan with sugar and lemon juice. Stir to combine. Let sit for 10 minutes, then bring to a boil, reduce heat to medium-low, and simmer until thickened, 10 to 15 minutes. Let cool.

For the Frosting: Melt chocolate chips in a microwave or double boiler. Let cool at room temperature, 10 minutes. Beat the shortening with an electric mixer until smooth. With the mixer on low, gradually add powdered sugar and vanilla. Add milk, 1 tablespoon at a time, and beat until the frosting reaches a spreadable consistency. Add melted chocolate and beat for 2 minutes or until light and fluffy.

Assemble the Cupcakes: Using a spoon, make a hole in the top of each cupcake and scoop out about 2 tablespoons of cake. Crumble into fine crumbs and reserve. Fill the holes with the filling. Frost with the frosting and top with the crumbled cake crumbs. Garnish with gummy worms.

Halloween Pumpkin Cupcakes

Makes 12 cupcakes

Ingredients:

For the Cupcakes:
1 cup pure pumpkin puree
⅓ cup mayonnaise or vegan mayonnaise, such as Vegenaise™
⅓ cup granulated sugar
⅓ cup light brown sugar, packed
¼ cup milk or dairy-free milk
1 tablespoon maple syrup
2 teaspoons pure vanilla extract
1¼ cups all-purpose flour (regular or gluten-free)
1 teaspoon baking powder
½ teaspoon baking soda
½ teaspoon kosher or fine sea salt

1 teaspoon ground cinnamon
¼ teaspoon freshly ground nutmeg
⅛ teaspoon ground cloves

For the Frosting:
8 ounces cream cheese or dairy-free alternative
½ cup butter or dairy-free alternative
2 tablespoons maple syrup
4 cups powdered sugar
Orange food coloring gel (optional)
Orange food decorating gel (optional for garnish)
6 green gumdrops, cut in half (optional for garnish)

Directions:

Preheat the oven to 350°F. Line a 12-cup standard muffin tin with paper liners.

Whisk together pumpkin puree, mayo, sugar, brown sugar, rice milk, maple syrup, and vanilla. In another bowl, whisk together flour, baking powder, baking soda, salt, cinnamon, nutmeg, and cloves. Add dry ingredients to the wet ingredients and whisk until fully combined.

Divide batter evenly among muffin cups, filling about two-thirds full. Bake for 18 to 22 minutes or until the tops of the cupcakes feel firm and a toothpick inserted into the center comes out clean. Let cool in the pan for 5 minutes, then transfer to a wire rack to finish cooling.

For the frosting, combine ingredients in a mixing bowl and beat, starting on low, to combine. Once the ingredients have combined, increase speed to medium-high and beat for 1 minute or until very smooth. If desired, add orange food coloring, a little at a time, until desired color is achieved.

Generously frost the cooled cupcakes and smooth the top of frosting into a round shape. Starting at the top of each cupcake, draw lines down to the cupcake liner with the orange decorating gel to form a spoke. Top each cupcake with half a gumdrop.

I will be the first to admit I am never going to win any pastry decorating contests. I can't do fancy piping and have no clue how to fashion things out of fondant.

But if I were able to make these look sort of like pumpkins with the help of food decorating gel and some gumdrop candies, your kids can, too!

Fourth of July Blueberry Cupcakes

Makes 12 cupcakes

Ingredients:

For the Cupcakes:
1½ cups plus 2 tablespoons all-purpose flour (regular or gluten-free)
1 teaspoon baking powder
½ teaspoon kosher or fine sea salt
½ cup unsalted butter, room temperature
1 cup granulated sugar
2 large eggs, room temperature
½ cup milk, room temperature
1 teaspoon pure vanilla extract
¾ cup blueberries, divided
4 tablespoons all-natural maraschino cherry juice
12 all-natural maraschino cherries with stems
Red, white, and blue sprinkles

For the Frosting:
½ cup unsalted butter, room temperature
⅛ teaspoon kosher or fine sea salt
2½ cups powdered sugar
½ teaspoon pure vanilla extract
2 teaspoons fresh lemon juice

Directions:

Preheat the oven to 350°F. Line 12 standard muffin cups with paper liners.

In a large mixing bowl, whisk together 1½ cups flour, baking powder, and salt.

In the bowl of an electric mixer, fitted with a paddle attachment, cream butter and sugar together on medium speed for 2 minutes or until light and fluffy. Scrape the sides of the bowl and add eggs, one at a time, mixing well and scraping down the sides of the bowl after each addition. Turn the mixer to low, add half the flour mixture, then milk, and finally the remaining flour mixture. Add vanilla extract and mix well. Scrape the sides and bottom of the bowl with a spatula to fully combine all ingredients.

Place ½ cup blueberries in a small mixing bowl, add 1 tablespoon flour, and toss together. Add ¾ cup of batter and gently fold blueberries into batter. Divide mixture among muffin cups. Smooth the batter with a small spatula and spread the batter all the way to the sides.

Place ¾ cup of batter in a small bowl, add remaining tablespoon of flour, and all-natural maraschino cherry juice. Mix well.

Gently spoon this batter on top of the blueberry layer. Smooth the batter and spread all the way to the sides. Spoon remaining batter on top of the cherry layer and spread as before.

Bake 20 to 25 minutes or until tops of cupcakes start to brown and a toothpick inserted in the center comes out clean. Let cool in the pan for 5 minutes. Transfer to a wire rack to finish cooling.

For the frosting, use an electric mixer to beat butter and salt on high until creamy. Add powdered sugar, vanilla, and lemon juice. Mix together, starting on low, then increasing speed until fully combined and fluffy.

Pipe or spread frosting onto cooled cupcakes and garnish with a cherry, blueberries, and sprinkles.

Cupcakes in a jar are perfect picnic treats! Just layer three cupcake halves with frosting in between, top with pistachios, and tie a pretty ribbon around the jar for a special presentation!

St. Paddy's Pistachio Cupcakes in a Jar

Makes 12 cupcakes in a jar or 18 standard cupcakes

Ingredients:

For the Cupcakes:
- 4 large eggs
- ¾ cup grape seed or other neutral-tasting oil
- ¾ cup water
- 1 (3.4-ounce) package instant pistachio pudding
- 1 (18-ounce) package white cake mix (regular or gluten-free)

For the Topping:
- 1 cup all-vegetable non-hydrogenated shortening, such as Spectrum™
- 1 teaspoon fresh lemon juice
- 2 teaspoons pure vanilla extract
- 4 cups powdered sugar
- 4 to 8 tablespoons milk or rice milk
- ¼ cup shelled, roasted, and salted pistachios, chopped

Directions:

Preheat the oven to 350°F. Line 18 standard muffin tins with paper liners.

In the bowl of an electric mixer, combine eggs, water, and oil. Beat on medium speed for 2 minutes. Turn off the mixer, add the pistachio pudding mix, and beat until combined. Turn the mixer to low and add cake mix gradually. Beat until just combined. With a rubber spatula, scrape the sides and bottom of the mixing bowl to make sure all ingredients are uniformly combined.

Divide batter among muffin tins, filling about two-thirds full. Bake 22 to 26 minutes or until cupcakes spring back when touched lightly and a toothpick inserted in the center comes out clean. Let cool completely. Remove liners from cupcakes and slice in half horizontally.

While the cupcakes are baking and cooling, make the frosting. Place shortening, lemon juice, and vanilla in an electric mixer fitted with a whisk attachment. Beat on high speed until very creamy. Turn off the mixer, add powdered sugar, and beat until combined, starting with the mixer on low and gradually increasing speed. With the mixer running, add rice milk, 1 tablespoon at a time, until frosting is creamy and spreadable. Once the desired consistency is achieved, beat on high speed for 1 minute.

For each cupcake in a jar, place a cupcake half in the bottom, pipe on or spoon in some frosting, add another cupcake half, another layer of frosting, one more cupcake half and one more layer of frosting. Be sure to use the bottom halves in the bottom of the jars and use the tops for the final layer. Top with chopped pistachios.

Easter Jelly Bean Cupcakes

Makes 12 cupcakes

Ingredients:

1 cup unsalted butter, room temperature
1 cup granulated sugar
2 large eggs
1½ cups all-purpose flour*
1½ teaspoons baking powder
½ teaspoon kosher or fine sea salt
½ cup buttermilk
Finely grated zest and juice of 1 lemon
1 teaspoon pure vanilla extract
36 jelly beans*

Frosting and decoration:
1 cup unsalted butter, room temperature
8 ounces cream cheese, room temperature
2 cups powdered sugar
Finely grated zest and juice of 1 lemon
1 teaspoon pure vanilla extract
Jelly beans*
Coconut flakes, optional
Watermelon ring gummies, optional*

*Can use regular or gluten-free.

Directions:

Preheat the oven to 350°F. Line a standard 12-cup muffin pan with cupcake liners.

In the bowl of a mixer, fitted with a paddle attachment, beat butter and sugar together until fluffy, about 3 minutes. Add eggs, one at a time, beating well after each addition.

In a separate bowl, whisk flour, baking powder, and salt. In another bowl, mix buttermilk, lemon zest/juice, and vanilla.

With the mixer on low, add half the flour mixture, the buttermilk mixture, then the remaining half of the flour. Mix just until combined. With a spatula, scrape the sides and bottom of the bowl to fully combine. Divide batter equally among muffin cups. Insert 3 jelly beans into each cupcake. Bake 25 to 30 minutes, until lightly brown and set. Cool in the pan 5 minutes. Transfer to a wire rack to finish cooling.

In the bowl of an electric mixer, fitted with a paddle attachment, beat butter and cream cheese together until smooth. Turn off the mixer. Sift in the powdered sugar, add lemon zest/juice, and vanilla. Start with the mixer on low, then gradually increase speed to high, and beat until smooth. If the frosting starts to look curdled, keep beating until smooth. Place in the fridge for 30 minutes to firm up.

Frost or pipe the frosting onto the cooled cupcakes. Sprinkle a few jelly beans on the frosting. For a nest, dip frosted cupcake into coconut and nestle 3 jelly beans in the center of each "nest." For flowers, place jelly beans in concentric circles from the center. Refrigerate until serving.

Baked Beverages

These drink-inspired cupcakes are bubbly, boozy, and baked to perfection. These cupcakes might not satisfy your thirst, but they are sure to satisfy your sweet tooth!

Shirley Temple Cupcakes

Makes 12 cupcakes

Ingredients:

For the Cupcakes:
1½ cups plus 1 tablespoon all-purpose flour (regular or gluten-free), divided
1 teaspoon baking powder
½ teaspoon kosher or fine sea salt
½ cup unsalted butter, room temperature
1 cup granulated sugar
2 large eggs, room temperature
½ cup 7-Up™, room temperature
1 teaspoon pure vanilla extract
1 tablespoon all-natural maraschino cherry juice
Red food coloring gel

For the Frosting:
½ cup unsalted butter, room temperature
1 large pinch of kosher or fine sea salt
2½ cups powdered sugar
½ teaspoon pure vanilla extract
1 teaspoon fresh lemon juice
1 tablespoon all-natural maraschino cherry juice
12 all-natural maraschino cherries, patted dry

Directions:

Preheat the oven to 350°F. Line 12 standard muffin cups with paper liners.

In a large mixing bowl, whisk 1½ cups of flour with the baking powder and salt.

In the bowl of an electric mixer, preferably fitted with a paddle attachment, cream the butter and sugar on medium-high speed for 2 minutes or until light and fluffy. Scrape down the sides of the bowl and add eggs, one at a time, mixing well and scraping down the bowl after each addition. Turn mixer to low and add half the flour mixture, then the 7-Up, and finally the rest of the flour mixture. Add vanilla extract and mix. Scrape the sides and bottom of the bowl well to ensure all ingredients are fully incorporated. Do not worry if the batter looks a little curdled.

Take ½ cup of the batter and put it in a small bowl. Add the remaining 1 tablespoon of flour, cherry juice, and enough red food coloring to turn the batter red. Stir well. Divide batter evenly between the muffin cups (about 1 big teaspoon per cup). Gently spoon the remaining batter on top of the red batter, trying not to mix the two colors but to keep them in layers.

Bake for 15 to 20 minutes or until the tops of the cupcakes are slightly springy and a toothpick inserted into the center comes out clean. Let cool in the pan for 5 minutes, then transfer to a wire rack to finish cooling. (The cupcakes will puff up a bit while cooking because of the 7-Up.)

Prepare the frosting while the cupcakes are cooling. Combine butter and salt in the bowl of an electric mixer, preferably fitted with a paddle attachment. Beat on high speed until creamy. Sift in the powdered sugar and mix on low until fully combined. Add vanilla, lemon juice, and cherry juice. Mix to combine. Frost the cupcakes and top with a cherry.

Irish Coffee Cupcakes

For the embellishments, I made chocolate straws by rolling thin straws in some melted semisweet chocolate and then freezing them. I also picked clovers from the garden and painted them with some melted chocolate. I have no idea if this is safe to do, so please don't eat the clover!

Makes 12 cupcakes

Ingredients:

For the Cupcakes:
½ cup granulated sugar
½ cup water
2 tablespoons instant espresso powder, divided
2 tablespoons good Irish Whiskey (or more)
1 cup all-purpose flour (regular or gluten-free)
1½ teaspoons baking powder
1 teaspoon kosher or fine sea salt
¾ cup unsalted butter, room temperature
¾ cup light brown sugar, packed
2 large eggs, room temperature
½ cup half-and-half or light cream, room temperature
1 teaspoon pure vanilla extract

For the Topping:
1½ cups heavy whipping cream
2 teaspoons granulated sugar

Directions:

Preheat the oven to 350°F. Line a standard muffin tin with paper liners.

In a small saucepan, stir together the granulated sugar and water. Bring to a boil over medium-high heat. Boil for 1 minute. Take off the heat and whisk in 1 tablespoon of instant espresso powder. Stir in the whiskey and let cool.

In a large mixing bowl, whisk together the flour, baking powder, salt, and remaining 1 tablespoon instant espresso powder.

In the bowl of an electric mixer, fitted with a paddle attachment, cream the butter and brown sugar on medium-high speed until fluffy, about 2 to 3 minutes. Add eggs, one at a time, mixing well and scraping the sides of the bowl after each addition. Turn the mixer to low and gradually add half the flour mixture, then the half-and-half, and finally the rest of the flour mixture. Blend until almost all the flour is mixed in. Add the vanilla and mix. With a large spatula, finish mixing the batter.

Divide the batter evenly between the muffin cups. Bake for 25 minutes or until a toothpick inserted in the center comes out clean. Let cool in the pan for 5 minutes and then spoon the coffee whiskey mixture evenly and slowly over the cupcakes. Let cool for 30 minutes in the pan, then transfer to a wire rack to finish cooling.

When the cupcakes are cool, make the topping. Whip the cream with 2 teaspoons of sugar and swirl on top of the cupcakes.

Old Fashioned Cupcakes

Makes 12 cupcakes

Ingredients:

For the Cupcakes:
½ cup unsalted butter, room temperature
1 cup granulated sugar
2 large eggs
1½ cups all-purpose flour (regular or gluten-free)
1 teaspoon baking powder
½ teaspoons baking soda
½ teaspoon kosher or fine sea salt
½ cup milk
¼ cup fresh orange juice
4 tablespoons whiskey
2 teaspoons pure vanilla extract
Zest of 1 orange, finely grated

For the Frosting:
1 cup unsalted butter, room temperature
3 to 4 cups powdered sugar
¼ teaspoon kosher or fine sea salt
¼ cup whiskey
6 dashes of bitters, such as Angostura™
Zest of 1 orange, finely grated
3 orange slices, cut in quarters
12 all-natural maraschino cherries, patted dry

Directions:

Preheat the oven to 350°F. Line a standard muffin tin with paper cupcake liners.

Cream the butter and sugar together in a mixer, preferably fitted with the paddle attachment, until light and fluffy, about 3 minutes. Scrape down the sides of the bowl and add the eggs, one at a time, beating well after each addition.

Combine flour, baking powder, baking soda, and salt in a mixing bowl and whisk.

Combine milk, orange juice, whiskey, and vanilla in a separate mixing bowl. It is OK if it looks a little curdled.

With the mixer on low, add half the flour mixture to the butter, then the milk mixture, and finally the rest of the flour. Add the orange zest and mix. Using a spatula, make sure the batter is fully mixed. Divide the batter into the prepared muffin tins and bake for 20 minutes or until they feel springy to the touch and a toothpick inserted into the center comes out clean. Let cool for 5 minutes in the pan, then transfer to a wire rack to finish cooling.

While the cupcakes cool, make the frosting. Combine the butter, 3 cups powdered sugar, and salt in a mixer, preferably fitted with the paddle attachment. Start the mixer on low, then increase the speed to medium and beat until fluffy, about 1 minute. Add the whiskey, bitters, and orange zest and mix. Add more powdered sugar, a little at a time, until the frosting is a spreadable consistency.

Frost the cooled cupcakes and garnish with a quartered orange slice and a cherry.

I love turning cocktails into cupcakes, and an Old Fashioned seemed like it would make a good candidate.

Boy, was that a good idea! The combination of orange, whiskey and bitters is indescribably delicious!

These boozy little cakes are not really fit for children. If there are kids around, just make a batch of orange cupcakes for them, omitting the whiskey from the cupcakes and the frosting.

These adults-only cupcakes are sure to entertain!

Manhattan Cupcakes

Makes 48 mini cupcakes

Ingredients:

For the Cupcakes:
2 cups all-purpose flour (regular or gluten-free)
½ teaspoon baking soda
1 teaspoon baking powder
½ teaspoon kosher or fine sea salt
¼ cup fresh orange juice
½ cup half-and-half or milk, room temperature
4 tablespoons bourbon whiskey
1 tablespoon sweet vermouth
½ cup unsalted butter, room temperature
1 cup granulated sugar
2 large eggs, room temperature
1 tablespoon finely grated orange zest
1 teaspoon finely grated lemon zest

For the Frosting:
½ cup unsalted butter, room temperature
4 cups powdered sugar
Large pinch of kosher or fine sea salt
5 tablespoons bourbon whiskey
1 tablespoon sweet vermouth
48 all-natural maraschino cherries with stems, drained and patted dry

Directions:

Preheat the oven to 350°F. Insert mini cupcake papers into 48 mini muffin cups.

In a large mixing bowl, whisk together the flour, baking soda, baking powder, and salt.

In a small mixing bowl, combine the orange juice, half-and-half or milk, bourbon, and sweet vermouth. It may look a little curdled; this is fine.

In an electric mixer, preferably fitted with a paddle attachment, cream the butter and sugar together on medium-high speed until fluffy, about 3 minutes. Scrape the bottom and sides of the bowl and add eggs, one at a time, blending well and scraping the bowl after each addition. Add orange zest and lemon zest and mix well. Turn the mixer to low and add one-third of the flour mixture, then half the orange juice mixture, half the remaining flour mixture, the rest of the orange juice mixture, and the rest of the flour. Mix until just combined. With a spatula, scrape the sides and bottom of the bowl to ensure all the ingredients are combined.

Spoon the batter into the muffin tins, filling about three-quarters full. Bake for 15 minutes or until the tops of the cupcakes spring back when lightly touched and a toothpick inserted in the center comes out clean. Let cool in the pans for 5 minutes, then transfer to a wire rack to finish cooling.

While the cupcakes cool, make the frosting. In a mixer, preferably fitted with a paddle attachment, cream the butter on medium-high speed until smooth and fluffy, about 1 minute. Sift in the powdered sugar, add the salt, and mix on low to combine. Scrape down the sides and bottom of the bowl, then add bourbon and vermouth. Mix on medium speed to combine. Frost the cooled cupcakes and top with a cherry.

Roy Rogers Cupcakes

A Roy Rogers is an old-fashioned drink that's similar to a Shirley Temple, except instead of 7-Up, it contains cola.

Makes 12 cupcakes

Ingredients:

For the Cupcakes:
1½ cups all-purpose flour (regular or dairy-free)
3 tablespoons unsweetened cocoa powder
½ teaspoon baking soda
½ teaspoon kosher or fine sea salt
½ cup buttermilk (or ½ cup dairy-free milk with ½ tablespoon white vinegar stirred in and left to sit for 5 minutes)
½ cup cola
¼ cup grenadine or maraschino cherry juice
2 teaspoons pure vanilla extract
½ cup unsalted butter (or dairy-free alternative), room temperature
¾ cup granulated sugar
1 large egg

For the Frosting:
1 cup heavy cream (or dairy-free whipped cream substitute)
2 teaspoons powdered sugar*
1 teaspoon pure vanilla extract*
12 maraschino cherries with stems

Omit if using dairy-free whipped cream.

Directions:

For the Cupcakes: Preheat the oven to 350°F. Line a standard muffin pan with paper cupcake liners.

In a mixing bowl, whisk together the flour, cocoa powder, baking soda, and salt. In another mixing bowl, whisk together the buttermilk, cola, grenadine, and vanilla and let sit until the cola stops fizzing.

In an electric mixer, preferably fitted with a paddle attachment, cream the butter and sugar together until light and fluffy, about 3 minutes. Add the egg and beat well. Turn the mixer to low and gradually add half the flour, then the buttermilk mixture, then the remaining flour. Using a spatula, scrape the sides and bottom of the bowl, making sure all ingredients are combined.

Divide batter evenly into the muffin tins and bake for 18 to 20 minutes or until a toothpick inserted in the center comes out clean. Let cool in the pan for 5 minutes, then transfer to a wire rack to finish cooling.

For the Frosting: Whip the cream with the powdered sugar and vanilla until soft peaks form. Pipe the frosting onto the cooled cupcakes and top with a maraschino cherry.

Margarita Cupcakes

Makes 12 cupcakes

Ingredients:

For the Cupcakes:
½ cup milk or dairy-free milk, room temperature
¼ cup fresh lime juice
1 teaspoon pure vanilla extract
1½ cups plus 2 tablespoons all-purpose flour (regular or gluten-free)
1 teaspoon baking powder
½ teaspoon kosher or fine sea salt
¼ teaspoon baking soda
½ cup organic vegetable shortening
¾ cup granulated sugar
2 large eggs, room temperature
Zest of 1 lime, finely grated
2 tablespoons tequila

For the Frosting:
1 cup organic vegetable shortening
2 tablespoons tequila
¼ cup fresh lime juice
Zest of 1 lime, finely grated
3 to 3½ cups powdered sugar

For the Garnish:
Finely grated lime zest
12 thinly sliced lime slices

Directions:

Preheat the oven to 350°F. Line a standard muffin pan with cupcake liners.

Combine the milk with ¼ cup lime juice and vanilla. Let sit for 5 minutes. It is OK if it looks curdled.

Whisk together the flour, baking powder, salt, and baking soda.

In an electric mixer, fitted with the paddle attachment, cream together ½ cup shortening with ¾ cup sugar. Beat in the eggs, one at a time, mixing well after each addition. Beat in the lime zest. Turn the mixer to low, add half the flour, the milk mixture, then the rest of the flour. Mix just until combined. With a spatula, scrape the sides and bottom of the bowl and make sure the batter is well combined. Divide the batter among the prepared muffin cups. Bake for 20 minutes or until a toothpick inserted into the center comes out clean. Brush the tops of the cupcakes with tequila, if desired. Let cool in the pan for 5 minutes, then transfer to a wire rack to finish cooling.

While the cupcakes bake and cool, make the frosting.

In a mixer, preferably fitted with a whisk attachment, beat together the shortening, tequila, lime juice, and lime zest. Add 3 cups powdered sugar and beat, starting at low speed, then increasing to medium-high until smooth and the consistency of butter cream. If too soft, add more powdered sugar, at little at a time.

Frost the cooled cupcakes and garnish with lime zest and a lime slice.

Dreamy Delights

These cupcakes are light and luscious, with surprisingly refreshing flavors. Featuring fruits, vegetables, and nuts, these cupcakes are the kinds of picture-perfect treats that dreams are made of.

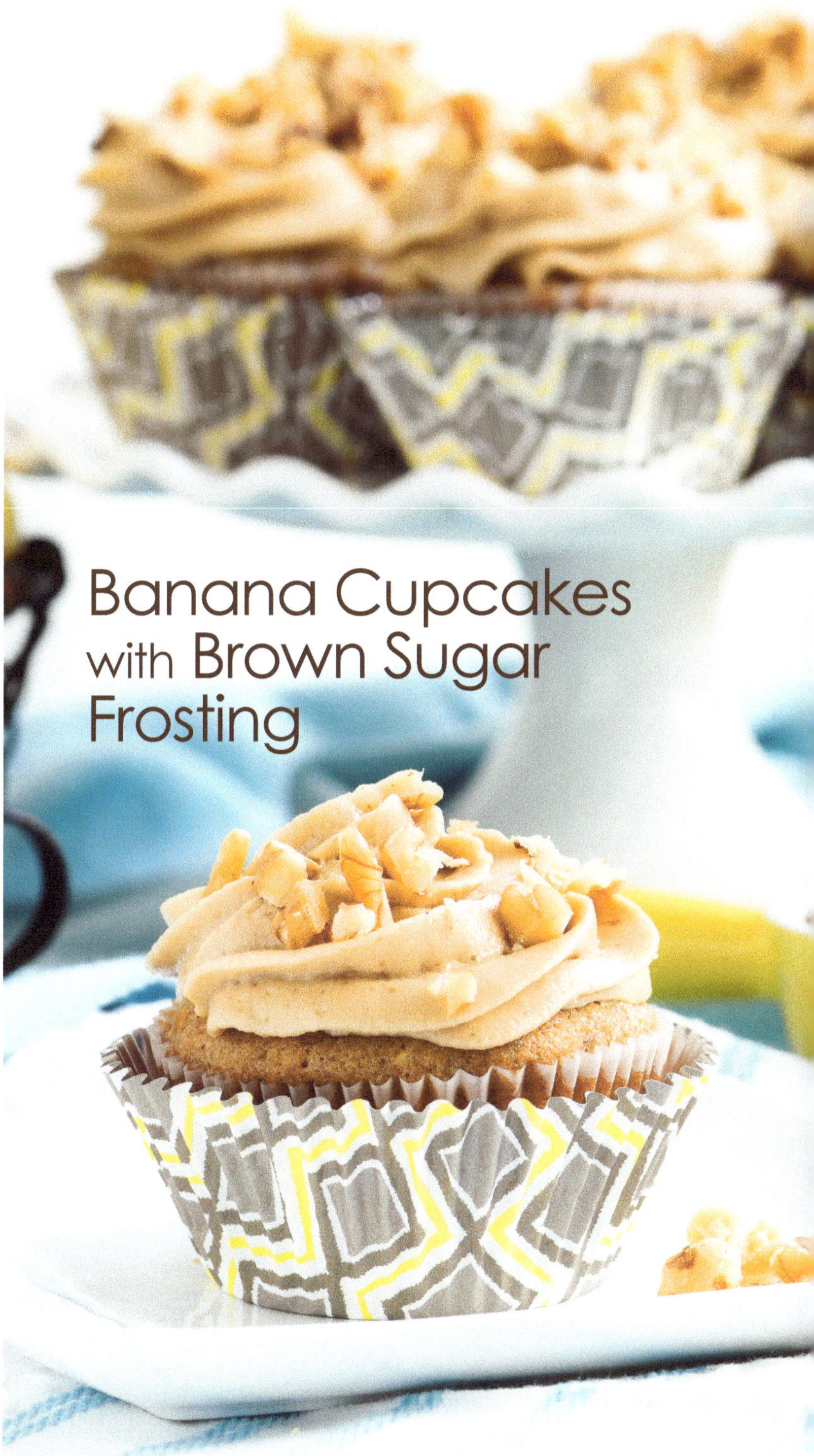

Makes 12 cupcakes

Ingredients:

For the Cupcakes:
1 cup all-purpose flour (regular or gluten-free)
½ teaspoon baking soda
½ teaspoon kosher or fine sea salt
½ cup unsalted butter, room temperature
½ cup granulated sugar
½ cup light brown sugar, packed
2 large eggs, room temperature
2 teaspoons pure vanilla extract
¼ cup sour cream
2 large ripe bananas, mashed
¾ cup chopped walnuts, plus more for garnish

For the Frosting:
½ cup unsalted butter, room temperature
8 ounces cream cheese, room temperature
1 cup light brown sugar, packed
¼ teaspoon kosher or fine sea salt

Directions:

For the Cupcakes: Preheat the oven to 350°F. Line a standard muffin tin with cupcake liners. In a mixing bowl, whisk flour, baking soda, and salt.

In the bowl of an electric mixer, fitted with a paddle attachment, cream butter and sugars on high speed until light and fluffy, about 3 minutes. Add eggs, one at a time, beating well after each addition. Add vanilla and beat well.

Turn the mixer on low and add half the flour mixture, then the sour cream, and the rest of the flour. Scrape the sides and bottom of the bowl with a spatula to combine well. Stir in the bananas and walnuts. Divide the batter evenly among the muffin tins and bake for 18 to 22 minutes or until a toothpick inserted in the center comes out clean. Let cool in the pan for 10 minutes, then transfer to a wire rack to finish cooling completely.

For the Frosting: In the bowl of an electric mixer, fitted with a paddle attachment, beat all the ingredients together on medium speed until smooth and creamy. Once the cupcakes are completely cooled, frost them and garnish with chopped walnuts, if desired.

Banana Cupcakes with Brown Sugar Frosting

Honey Orange Cupcakes

Makes 12 standard or 24 mini cupcakes

Ingredients:

For the Cupcakes:
Nonstick cooking spray (regular or gluten-free)
3 large eggs, separated
2½ cups finely ground blanched almond flour
½ teaspoon baking soda
½ teaspoon kosher or fine sea salt
4 tablespoons honey
¼ cup grape seed or other neutral-tasting oil
1 teaspoon pure vanilla extract
2 tablespoons fresh orange juice

For the Frosting:
⅔ cup pure vegetable shortening
4 tablespoons honey
4 tablespoons fresh orange juice
2 tablespoon orange zest, finely grated

Directions:

For the Cupcakes: Preheat the oven to 350°F. Insert cupcake liners into a 12-cup standard muffin pan or 24-cup mini muffin pan.

In a bowl, whip the egg whites to stiff peaks.

In another mixing bowl, combine the egg yolks, almond flour, baking soda, salt, honey, oil, vanilla, and orange juice. Beat with a mixer until smooth and fully combined. Fold the beaten egg whites into the mixture until the batter is no longer streaky. Divide the batter evenly among the prepared muffin tins and bake for 20 to 22 minutes for standard cupcakes or 10 to 12 minutes for minis or until a toothpick inserted into the center comes out clean. Cool in the pan for 5 minutes, then transfer to a wire rack to finish cooling.

For the Frosting: Combine the shortening, honey, orange juice, and orange zest in a medium mixing bowl and beat with a hand-held mixer until smooth and fluffy. Your mixture may become curdled looking; if so, just keep beating until it is smooth. Frost the cooled cupcakes.

Italian Cream Cupcakes

Makes 12 cupcakes

Ingredients:

2 large eggs, separated
1 cup all-purpose flour (regular or gluten-free)
½ teaspoon kosher or fine sea salt
½ teaspoon baking soda
½ cup buttermilk
3 tablespoons maraschino cherry juice
¼ cup pure vegetable shortening, room temperature
12 tablespoons unsalted butter, room temperature, divided
¾ cup granulated sugar
2 teaspoons pure vanilla extract, divided
¾ cup chopped pecans, divided
1½ cups coconut flakes, divided
8 ounces cream cheese, room temperature
3½ to 4½ cups powdered sugar
12 maraschino cherries with stems, patted dry

Directions:

Preheat the oven to 350°F. Line a standard 12-cup muffin pan with paper liners.

In a bowl, beat the egg whites with a hand-held mixer until stiff. In a separate bowl, whisk flour, salt, and baking soda. In another bowl, mix buttermilk and cherry juice.

In the bowl of an electric mixer, fitted with a paddle attachment, cream the shortening, 4 tablespoons butter, and sugar together until light and fluffy, about 3 minutes. Add 1 teaspoon vanilla and mix well. Add egg yolks, one at a time, mixing well after each addition. With the mixer on low, add half the flour mixture, then the buttermilk, and remaining flour. Using a spatula, scrape the bottom and sides of the bowl well to fully combine. Fold in the beaten egg whites. Fold in ½ cup pecans and 1 cup coconut. Divide batter among the muffin tins and bake for 15 minutes or until the cupcakes spring back when lightly touched and a toothpick inserted in the center comes out clean. Let cool in the pan for 5 minutes, then transfer to a wire rack to finish cooling.

Meanwhile, make the frosting. In the bowl of an electric mixer, fitted with a paddle attachment, beat the remaining 8 tablespoons butter and the cream cheese until smooth. Add 1 teaspoon vanilla and 3½ cups powdered sugar and beat until combined. Add more powdered sugar, as necessary, until the frosting is thick and smooth. Frost the cupcakes and sprinkle with the remaining ¼ cup pecans and coconut. Top each cupcake with a cherry.

Lemon-Lime Cupcakes

Makes 12 cupcakes

Ingredients:

2 organic lemons
2 organic limes
8 tablespoons unsalted butter, room temperature
½ cup granulated sugar
3 large eggs, room temperature
½ teaspoon pure vanilla extract
1 cup plus 2 tablespoons all-purpose flour (regular or gluten-free)
½ teaspoon baking powder
Scant ½ teaspoon kosher or fine sea salt
1½ cups powdered sugar, sifted

For the Garnish:
4 organic lemons or limes
3 cups granulated sugar
2 cups water

Directions:

Preheat the oven to 325°F. Line 12 cups of a standard muffin pan with paper liners.

Finely zest the lemons and limes and mix the zests together, reserving ¼ teaspoon for the glaze. Juice the lemons and limes and mix the juices together, reserving 3 tablespoons of the juice for the glaze, and saving the rest for another use.

In the bowl of an electric mixer, fitted with a paddle attachment, cream the butter and granulated sugar on medium speed until very light and fluffy, about 5 minutes. Turn the speed to low and add the eggs, one at a time, mixing well until each egg is fully incorporated, and scraping down the sides of the bowl with a spatula after each addition. Add the vanilla and lemon/lime zest and mix well.

In a separate large mixing bowl, whisk together the flour, baking powder, and salt. With the mixer on low speed, gradually add the flour mixture into the butter mixture. With a spatula, scrape down the sides and bottom of the bowl to ensure the batter is mixed well. Divide the batter among the muffin cups.

Bake for 20 to 25 minutes, or until springy on top and a toothpick inserted in the center comes out clean. Let cool in the pan for 10 minutes, then transfer to a wire rack to cool completely.

When completely cooled, whisk together the powdered sugar, 3 tablespoons lemon/lime juice, and the reserved ¼ teaspoon of lemon/lime zest until completely smooth.

Set the rack with the cooled cupcakes on a rimmed baking sheet. Spoon the glaze onto the cupcakes and refrigerate until the glaze hardens, about 30 minutes. Garnish with candied peels, if desired.

For the Garnish: With a citrus zester, peel off thin strips of the peel from the lemons/limes. In a saucepan, combine 2 cups of sugar with the water and bring to a boil. Add the peels and boil for 20 minutes. Place 1 cup of sugar in a bowl. Strain the peels from the liquid, add to the sugar, and toss to coat. Separate the candied peels and let dry on waxed paper or foil for several hours.

Julian's Carrot Cupcakes with Cream Cheese Frosting

Makes 12 cupcakes

Ingredients:

For the Cupcakes:
1 cup granulated sugar
1 teaspoon pure vanilla extract
¾ cup grape seed or other neutral-tasting vegetable oil
1 tablespoon fresh orange juice
1½ teaspoons finely grated orange zest
2 large eggs, room temperature
1 cup all-purpose flour (regular or gluten-free)
1 teaspoon ground cinnamon
½ teaspoon baking soda
1 teaspoon baking powder
¾ teaspoon kosher or fine sea salt
½ pound carrots, grated (about 1½ cups)
½ cup raisins
½ cup walnuts, optional

For the Frosting:
6 ounces cream cheese or dairy-free alternative, room temperature
8 tablespoons unsalted butter or dairy-free buttery sticks, room temperature
⅛ teaspoon kosher or fine sea salt
1 teaspoon pure vanilla extract
½ pound powdered sugar

For the Garnish:
3 medium oranges (about 1½ pounds)
2 cups granulated sugar, divided
1 cup water

Directions:

For the Cupcakes: Preheat the oven to 350°F. Line 12 cups of a standard muffin pan with paper liners.

In the bowl of an electric mixer, fitted with the paddle attachment, beat together the sugar, vanilla, oil, orange juice, and zest on medium speed. Reduce speed to low and add eggs, one at a time, mixing well and scraping down the sides of the bowl after each addition.

In a large mixing bowl, whisk together flour, cinnamon, baking soda, baking powder, and salt. With the mixer on low, add half the flour mixture to the wet ingredients. Add carrots, raisins, and walnuts (if using) to the remaining flour mixture and toss well to coat. Add to the batter and mix well with a spatula, making sure to scrape the sides and bottom of the bowl. Divide batter evenly among the prepared muffin cups.

Bake for 35 to 45 minutes or until a toothpick inserted in the center comes out clean. Let cool in the pan for 10 minutes, then transfer to a wire rack to finish cooling. When completely cool, frost with cream cheese frosting and garnish with candied orange zest, if desired.

For the Frosting: In the bowl of an electric mixer, fitted with the paddle attachment, beat together the cream cheese, butter, salt, and vanilla on medium speed. Turn the mixer off and sift in the powdered sugar. Turn the mixer on low and beat until smooth.

For the Garnish: With a citrus zester, peel off thin strips of peel from the oranges. In a saucepan, combine 1 cup sugar with water and bring to a boil. Add the orange peel and boil for 20 minutes. Place 1 cup sugar in a bowl. Strain the orange peel from the liquid, add to the sugar, and toss to coat. Separate the candied peels and let dry on waxed paper or foil for several hours.

When I first asked my 3-year-old grandson, Julian, if he would like some carrot cake, he laughed hysterically and thought I was making a great joke! I realized that since carrots are vegetables, the idea of carrot cake was as funny to him as, say, string bean cake. He got over his prejudice and now carrot cake is his favorite ... especially carrot cupcakes!

Homemade from a Box

We all need cooking shortcuts from time to time. These recipes help simplify your party plans by taking boxed cake mixes and transforming them into unique creations – without the use of the stand mixer!

Snickerdoodle Cupcakes

Makes 12 cupcakes

Ingredients:

For the Cupcakes:
2 teaspoons ground cinnamon, divided
6 teaspoons granulated sugar
1 box white cake mix (regular or gluten-free), plus ingredients to make it
1 teaspoon pure vanilla extract

For the Frosting:
½ cup unsalted butter (or dairy-free alternative)
4 cups powdered sugar
1 teaspoon ground cinnamon
1 pinch kosher or fine sea salt
2 teaspoon pure vanilla extract
2 to 6 tablespoons milk (or dairy-free milk)

Directions:

Combine 1 teaspoon cinnamon and 6 teaspoons sugar in a small bowl. Set aside.

Combine cake mix and ingredients called for on the package. Add vanilla and 1 teaspoon cinnamon. Whisk until combined. Divide batter among paper-lined muffin tins. Sprinkle about ¼ teaspoon of the cinnamon-sugar mixture on each cupcake. Bake according to package directions. Let cool.

Meanwhile, make the frosting. In the bowl of an electric mixer, preferably fitted with a paddle attachment, beat the butter until smooth. Add powdered sugar, cinnamon, salt, vanilla, and 2 tablespoons milk. Start with the mixer on low and combine. Gradually add more milk until the mixture becomes spreadable. Turn the mixer to medium-high and beat for 30 seconds or until very creamy.

Frost the cooled cupcakes. Sprinkle with the remaining cinnamon-sugar mixture. Insert a cinnamon stick into each.

For the chocolate cake mix called for in this recipe, you may want to try Carol's Gluten Free® Chocolate Cake Mix (available on Amazon and simplygluten-free.com).

Chocolate Coconut Pecan Cupcakes

Makes 12 cupcakes

Ingredients:

1 package chocolate cake mix (regular or gluten-free), plus ingredients to make it
½ cup coconut milk or heavy cream
4 cups plus ⅓ cup powdered sugar, divided
1⅓ cups plus ¼ cup sweetened coconut flakes, divided
⅓ cup chopped pecans
2 teaspoons pure vanilla extract, divided
¾ teaspoon pure almond extract, divided
8 ounces cream cheese, room temperature
8 ounces unsalted butter, room temperature
⅛ teaspoon kosher or fine sea salt

Directions:

Mix and bake cupcakes according to package directions.

Let cool in the pans for 10 minutes, then transfer to a wire rack to finish cooling. Cut a circular cone of cake from the top of each cupcake. Cut tops off the cones and reserve the tops.

In a small saucepan, combine milk and ⅓ cup powdered sugar. Bring to a boil. Cook until thickened, about 1 minute. Stir in 1⅓ cups coconut flakes, pecans, 1 teaspoon vanilla, and ¼ teaspoon almond extract. Let cool. Fill cupcakes with this mixture and top with the reserved pieces of cake.

In a dry skillet over medium heat, toast remaining ¼ cup coconut until golden brown and fragrant. Let cool.

In an electric mixer, fitted with a paddle attachment, combine cream cheese and butter and beat until very smooth. Add 4 cups powdered sugar and, starting on low then increasing to high, beat in the sugar until fully incorporated. Beat in the remaining teaspoon vanilla and ½ teaspoon almond extract. Frost the cupcakes and top with toasted coconut.

Chocolate Strawberry Cupcakes

Makes 12 cupcakes

Ingredients:

For the Cupcakes:
1 box chocolate cake mix (regular or gluten-free), plus ingredients to make it
2 teaspoons pure vanilla extract
1 teaspoon instant espresso powder

For the Filling:
2 pints fresh strawberries
⅓ cup sugar
1 tablespoon fresh lemon juice

For the Frosting:
2 cups cold heavy cream
1 tablespoon pure vanilla extract
3 tablespoons powdered sugar

Directions:

Mix the cupcakes according to package directions, with the addition of vanilla and espresso powder. Pour into a standard 12-cup muffin pan and bake according to package directions. Let cool completely.

While the cupcakes are baking and cooling, reserve a few strawberries for garnish, slice the rest, and mix with ⅓ cup sugar and the lemon juice. Let sit for 15 to 20 minutes, tossing occasionally. Lightly mash the strawberries with a fork.

Cut a hole about as wide as a quarter and about ½ inch or so deep into the top of each cooled cupcake. Spoon the strawberry mixture into the holes (you can reserve some of the strawberries and syrup to drizzle on top of the frosted cupcakes, if desired).

Whip the cream with the vanilla and powdered sugar until it forms peaks. Frost each cupcake with the whipped cream. Slice the reserved strawberries and garnish.

Flower Cupcakes

Makes 12 cupcakes

Ingredients:

12 small terra cotta flower pots (about 2 inches)
1 box chocolate cake mix, plus ingredients to make it*
Chocolate frosting*
1 cup crushed chocolate cookie crumbs*
12 lollipop sticks
12 watermelon or peach ring gummies*
White decorating icing (not gel)
Jelly beans and gummy worms*

Note: I used gluten-free, organic gummies and jelly beans from Surf Sweets™ to avoid corn syrup and artificial colors/flavors.

*Can use regular or gluten-free.

Directions:

Bake the cupcakes per package directions. If using terra cotta pots, fill two-thirds full with batter before baking. Let cool completely.

Spread a layer of frosting on each cupcake. Place crushed cookie crumbs on a small plate and dip frosting into the crumbs.

For the flowers, place icing on jelly beans and "glue" them to the candy rings. Insert a lollipop stick into the ring and insert the flower into the cupcake. Add gummy worms to the pot and serve.

Graveyard Cupcakes

Makes 12 cupcakes

Ingredients:

1 box chocolate cake mix, plus ingredients to make it*
1 (16-ounce) tub chocolate frosting*
12 chocolate sandwich cream cookies (such as Oreos™ or gluten-free Kinnitoos™)
White decorating icing*
Gummy worms and jelly beans*

*Can use regular or gluten-free.

Directions:

Mix and bake the cupcakes according to package directions. Let cool in the pans for 5 minutes. Transfer to a wire rack to finish cooling. Frost the cooled cupcakes.

Twist the sandwich cookies to separate into two halves. Scrape the frosting from the middle and discard. Cut the bottom third off of half the cookies. Place the smaller cut portions in a plastic food storage bag along with the remaining cookie halves. Using a rolling pin, crush the cookies until they resemble dirt. Sprinkle the crumbs on top of the frosted cupcakes.

With the decorating icing, write on the side of the cut cookies that the filling was on. Make sure the flat side of the cookie is the bottom of the tombstone. You can write things like RIP, Boo, or people's initials. Stick the cookies into the frosting and prop up the back with a toothpick, if needed. Cut gummy worms in half and stick a half into each side of the cupcakes. Place 2 jelly bean "grubs" on each cupcake.

These cupcakes were made and photographed by my granddaughter, Milla.

Cherry Heart Cupcakes

Makes 12 cupcakes

Ingredients:

For the Garnish:
12 all-natural maraschino cherries with stems
⅓ cup dark chocolate chips

For the Cupcakes:
1 box chocolate cake mix (regular or gluten-free), plus ingredients to make it
1 teaspoon pure vanilla extract

For the Frosting/Filling:
8 ounces cream cheese, room temperature
½ cup unsalted butter, room temperature
Pinch of kosher or fine sea salt
1 teaspoon pure vanilla extract
2 tablespoons maraschino cherry juice
2 cups (or more) powdered sugar
12 all-natural maraschino cherries without stems

For the chocolate cake mix called for in this recipe, you may want to try Carol's Gluten Free® Chocolate Cake Mix (available on Amazon and simplygluten-free.com).

Directions:

First, make the chocolate covered cherries for garnish. Line a baking sheet with waxed or parchment paper. Place the cherries on some paper towels and let them dry. Melt the chocolate chips in the microwave until they are almost all melted, about 1½ to 2 minutes. Stir the chocolate until it is all melted and glossy. Dip the cherries into the chocolate and place on the baking sheet, pressing down a little to create a flat surface. Refrigerate for 30 minutes or until the chocolate has hardened.

Combine the cake mix with the ingredients called for on the package, plus vanilla extract. Bake according to package directions. Let cool for 5 minutes in the pan, then transfer to a cooling rack to finish cooling.

While the cupcakes cool, make the frosting/filling. Beat the cream cheese, butter, salt, vanilla, and cherry juice together until blended. Sift in 2 cups powdered sugar and mix to combine. If the frosting seems too soft, beat in a little more to stiffen it. The mixture should be a little thicker than heavily whipped cream.

Take about ½ cup of frosting and put it in a plastic food storage bag. Snip off the end of the bag and pipe the mixture into the cupcakes. Refrigerate the rest of the frosting until time to finish the cupcakes.

To assemble the cupcakes, cut an inverted cone out of the top of each cupcake about the size of a nickel. Remove the cone and save it. With the end of a wooden spoon (or your finger) gently push the hole in the cupcake to widen it. Pipe about 1 teaspoon of frosting into the hole. Place a cherry on the frosting and then pipe in a little more frosting to cover the cherry. Cut the end off the reserved cone and place it back on top of the cupcake to cover the hole. Repeat with remaining cupcakes. Frost the cupcakes and place a chocolate-covered cherry on top of each.

Index

A
About the Author, 2

B
Banana Cupcakes with Brown Sugar Frosting, 63
Bloody Surprise Cupcakes, 41

C
Carol's Black Forest Cupcakes, 7
Cherry Heart Cupcakes, 76

Cherry
Carol's Black Forest Cupcakes, 7
Cherry Heart Cupcakes, 76
Chocolate Almond Christmas Cupcakes, 40
Chocolate Cherry Flourless Mini Cupcakes, 10
Fourth of July Blueberry Cupcakes, 45
Italian Cream Cupcakes, 65
Manhattan Cupcakes, 65
Mini Cherry Brownie Cupcakes, 20
Old Fashioned Cupcakes, 54
Roy Rogers Cupcakes, 66
Shirley Temple Cupcakes, 50

Chocolate
Bloody Surprise Cupcakes, 41
Carol's Black Forest Cupcakes, 7
Cherry Heart Cupcakes, 76
Chocolate Almond Christmas Cupcakes, 40
Chocolate Cherry Flourless Mini Cupcakes, 10
Chocolate Coconut Pecan Cupcakes, 72
Chocolate Ginger Bites, 14
Chocolate Raspberry Cupcakes, 13
Chocolate Strawberry Cupcakes, 73
Cookies & Cream No-Bake Cupcakes, 38
Flourless Peanut Butter Chocolate Cupcakes, 21
Flower Cupcakes, 74
German Chocolate Cupakes, 8
Graveyard Cupcakes, 75
Mexican Chocolate Cupcakes, 11
Mini Cherry Brownie Cupcakes, 20
Mint Chocolate Chip Cupcakes, 17
Peanut Butter-Filled Chocolate Cupcakes, 18

Chocolate Almond Christmas Cupcakes, 40
Chocolate Cherry Flourless Mini Cupcakes, 10
Chocolate Coconut Pecan Cupcakes, 72
Chocolate Ginger Bites, 14
Chocolate Raspberry Cupcakes, 13
Chocolate Strawberry Cupcakes, 73
Cinnamon Apple Cupcakes, 37
Cookies & Cream No-Bake Cupcakes, 38

D
Dairy-Free Recipes
Bloody Surprise Cupcakes, 41
Chocolate Almond Christmas Cupcakes, 40
Cinnamon Apple Cupcakes, 37
Flourless Peanut Butter Chocolate Cupcakes, 21
German Chocolate Cupcakes, 8
Graveyard Cupcakes, 75
Halloween Pumpkin Cupcakes, 42
Honey Orange Cupcakes, 64
Julian's Carrot Cupcakes
    with Cream Cheese Frosting, 68
Margarita Cupcakes, 61
Mexican Chocolate Cupcakes, 11
Roy Rogers Cupcakes, 66
Snickerdoodle Cupcakes, 71
St. Paddy's Pistachio Cupcakes in a Jar, 47
Strawberry Cupcakes, 29

E
Easter Jelly Bean Cupcakes, 48

Egg-Free Recipes
Bloody Surprise Cupcakes, 41
Cookies & Cream No-Bake Cupcakes, 38
German Chocolate Cupcakes, 8
Halloween Pumpkin Cupcakes, 42
Mexican Chocolate Cupcakes, 11
Strawberry Cupcakes, 29

F
Famous Red Velvet Cupcakes, 26
Flourless Peanut Butter Chocolate Cupcakes, 21
Flower Cupcakes, 74
Fourth of July Blueberry Cupcakes, 45

G
German Chocolate Cupcakes, 8
Graveyard Cupcakes, 75

Gluten-Free Recipes
(All recipes can be made gluten-free.)

H
Halloween Pumpkin Cupcakes, 42
Honey Orange Cupcakes, 64

I
Italian Cream Cupcakes, 65
Irish Coffee Cupcakes, 53

J
Julian's Carrot Cupcakes
    with Cream Cheese Frosting, 68
Jumbo Coconut Cupcakes, 25

L
Lemon-Lime Cupcakes, 67

M
Manhattan Cupcakes, 65
Margarita Cupcakes, 61
Mexican Chocolate Cupcakes, 11
Mini Cherry Brownie Cupcakes, 20
Mint Chocolate Chip Cupcakes, 17

N
Nut-Free Recipes
Bloody Surprise Cupcakes, 41
Carol's Black Forest Cupcakes, 7
Cherry Heart Cupcakes, 76
Chocolate Cherry Flourless Mini Cupcakes, 10
Chocolate Ginger Bites, 14
Chocolate Raspberry Cupcakes, 13
Chocolate Strawberry Cupcakes, 73
Cinnamon Apple Cupcakes, 37
Cookies & Cream No-Bake Cupcakes, 38
Easter Jelly Bean Cupcakes, 48
Famous Red Velvet Cupcakes, 26
Flourless Peanut Butter Chocolate Cupcakes, 21
Flower Cupcakes, 74
Fourth of July Blueberry Cupcakes, 45
Graveyard Cupcakes, 75
Halloween Pumpkin Cupcakes, 42
Irish Coffee Cupcakes, 53
Julian's Carrot Cupcakes
    with Cream Cheese Frosting, 68
Lemon-Lime Cupcakes, 67
Manhattan Cupcakes, 65
Margarita Cupcakes, 61
Mexican Chocolate Cupcakes, 11
Mint Chocolate Chip Cupcakes, 17
Old Fashioned Cupcakes, 54
Roy Rogers Cupcakes, 66
Salted Caramel Cupcakes, 35
Shirley Temple Cupcakes, 50
Snickerdoodle Cupcakes, 71
Strawberry Cupcakes, 29
Strawberry Shortcake Cupcakes, 30
Very Vanilla Cupcakes, 23

O
Old Fashioned Cupcakes, 54

P
Peanut Butter & Jelly Cupcakes, 33
Peanut Butter-Filled Chocolate Cupcakes, 18

R
Refined Sugar-Free Recipes
Chocolate Raspberry Cupcakes, 13
Cinnamon Apple Cupcakes, 37
Honey Orange Cupcakes, 64
Salted Caramel Cupcakes, 35

Roy Rogers Cupcakes, 66

S
Salted Caramel Cupcakes, 35
Shirley Temple Cupcakes, 50
Snickerdoodle Cupcakes, 71
St. Paddy's Pistachio Cupcakes in a Jar, 47
Strawberry Cupcakes, 29
Strawberry Shortcake Cupcakes, 30

V
Vegan Recipes
Bloody Surprise Cupcakes, 41
German Chocolate Cupcakes, 8
Halloween Pumpkin Cupcakes, 42
Mexican Chocolate Cupcakes, 11
Strawberry Cupcakes, 29

Very Vanilla Cupcakes, 23

www.ingramcontent.com/pod-product-compliance
Lightning Source LLC
Chambersburg PA
CBHW042009150426
43195CB00002B/67